The Edupreneur's Side Hustle Handbook

10 Successful Educators Share Their Top Tips

Edited by Lisa Dunnigan and Tosha Wright

Routledge
Taylor & Francis Group

NEW YORK AND LONDON

First published 2020
by Routledge
52 Vanderbilt Avenue, New York, NY 10017

and by Routledge
2 Park Square, Milton Park, Abingdon, Oxon, OX14 4RN

Routledge is an imprint of the Taylor & Francis Group, an informa business

Library of Congress Cataloging-in-Publication Data
Names: Dunnigan, Lisa, editor. | Wright, Tosha, editor.
Title: The edupreneur's side hustle handbook : 10 successful educators
    share their top tips / edited by Lisa Dunnigan and Tosha Wright.
Description: New York, NY : Routledge, 2020. | Includes
    bibliographical references. |
Identifiers: LCCN 2019059780 (print) | LCCN 2019059781 (ebook) |
    ISBN 9780367354572 (hardback) | ISBN 9780367354565 (paperback) |
    ISBN 9780429331510 (ebook)
Subjects: LCSH: Teachers—Supplementary employment. |
    Entrepreneurship.
Classification: LCC LB2844.1.S86 E48 2020 (print) | LCC LB2844.1.S86
    (ebook) | DDC 371.1—dc23
LC record available at https://lccn.loc.gov/2019059780
LC ebook record available at https://lccn.loc.gov/2019059781

ISBN: 978-0-367-35457-2 (hbk)
ISBN: 978-0-367-35456-5 (pbk)
ISBN: 978-0-429-33151-0 (ebk)

Typeset in Palatino
by Apex CoVantage, LLC

Printed in Canada

Contents

Meet the Authors

Lisa Dunnigan has over 30 years of experience as an educator. Lisa was a single parent when she had Elise and Tosha at the age of 18. She was determined not to let her pregnancy get in the way of her education. She was able to receive her college degree three times. During her career, she has been a seventh-grade teacher at Carrollton Junior High School in Carrollton, Georgia. Upon later getting married, she moved the family to Gainesville, Georgia, where she taught fourth grade. As the twins were starting high school, they made a final move to Douglasville, Georgia, where Lisa's career continued to grow. During her early tenure at Douglas County Schools, she held positions of increasing responsibility, including school counselor, assistant principal, and principal. As an elementary school principal, Lisa was recognized often. Additionally, because of the multiple instructional gains made by her staff and students during her tenure, Lisa received several additional school achievement awards. In 2012, Lisa became the Title I Executive Director for the Douglas County School System. In February 2020, she plans to retire and work full-time for her company, The Wright Stuff Chics, Inc.

Tosha Wright began her career teaching kindergarten outside of Atlanta in 2005. She has taught first grade in Ohio and Virginia and was a curriculum and International Baccalaureate (IB) coordinator in Pennsylvania for five years. Tosha moved back to Georgia in 2018 to become an assistant principal at a high school outside of Atlanta. She is the co-owner of The Wright Stuff Chics, Inc., co-founder of the Teach Your Heart Out Conferences, and CEO of The Pink Santa Hat Movement, Incorporated.

Eric Crouch is a fifth-grade teacher in Columbus, Georgia. He began teaching in 2011 and has been recognized nationally with the Milken Educator Award, a $25,000 prize for outstanding teaching, and in 2019 was recognized internationally by the Varkey Foundation as one of the "Top 50 Teachers in the World" by the Global Teacher Prize. In 2018, after Hurricane Michael hit a nearby community, Crouch and his students traveled to Bay County School District and interviewed teachers, principals, and others impacted by the hurricane. The students helped edit a documentary that would be seen and shared thousands of times over social media. As a result of the outreach and video, Bay County School District received nearly $2 million in donations. He has used his background in photography and film to teach his students how to change the world. In 2017, his students changed the lives of 56 Kenyan students when their marketing strategy raised enough money to save a school in rural Kenya. Eric speaks all across the country at Teach Your Heart Out about how to create and share work that matters. He and his students can be followed on Instagram @adventureswithmrc.

Kristen Donegan began teaching first grade in Orange County, California, in 2005. While teaching full-time, she also earned her master's degree in education with an emphasis in reading. Additionally, she holds a reading specialist certificate. Kristen presented professional development for her district for several years before creating her website, www. easyteachingtools.com, in 2008. She taught on O'ahu and eventually found her forever teaching home in San Diego with her husband and new baby. She and her team run Easy Teaching Tools Inc. full time while continuing to teach professional development (PD) online and across the country.

Michelle Ferré began her teaching career in 2014 and has since taught second and fourth grade in different districts across the state of Maryland. In addition to teaching in the classroom, Michelle has served her school as an e-coach to help teachers integrate educational technology into their instruction. She began documenting her life as a teacher and sharing her organizational, productivity, and instructional strategies on her YouTube channel, Pocketful of Primary, in 2016. She aims to assist and support new teachers entering the field through the tips shared in her videos. Michelle also creates and sells various templates and educational resources for teachers in her Pocketful of Primary TpT store.

Cynthia Frias is the founder of Social One Marketing, a boutique agency that assists businesses in increasing their social media presence by building strategic and insightful content. In 2011, she started a fashion jewelry business via internet only, which propelled her into a successful social media marketing world. She has worked passionately in the field for over eight years as a social media manager and trainer. Her clients are some of today's most popular and influential social media personalities. Cynthia lives in San Diego, California, with her three beautiful daughters and when she's not working on social media content, you will find her on her yoga mat.

Jen Jones began her career in education in 1994 teaching in California. She has taught in Florida and now lives in North Carolina. She has taught first, second, third, fourth, fifth, and eighth grades. She was trained in Reading Recovery in 1997–1998. She was trained in Fountas & Pinnell Guided Reading in 2000. She was a literacy trainer for the Florida Reading Initiative. She was a literacy coach, Instructional Resource Teacher (IRT), and school improvement chair in a large district in North Carolina. She owns a literacy professional development company, Hello Literacy, and trains teachers in schools and districts throughout the United States, Canada, and Australia. Her Hello Literacy Teachers Pay Teachers (TpT) store is at www.hellojenjones.com and more information about her training and workshops can be found at www.helloliteracy.com.

Kisha Mitchell began her teaching career in 2004. She has been a sixth and seventh-grade language arts teacher, graduation coach, and an assistant high school and middle school principal. Kisha is currently an elementary school principal. She is the author of two children's books, *Brown Girl, Brown Girl, What Do You See?* and *Brown Boy, You Must Believe!* Kisha co-hosts a podcast on iTunes called Sweet Tea and Sunshine, where she looks to inspire married couples to know that they are married, and not dead! She spearheaded the integration of several diversity and acceptance programs and workshops in districts in Georgia. She has also developed her very own mentoring curriculum called *The Kid's Guide to L.O.V.E. (Lifting Ourselves by Valuing Everyone)*, which gives children a peek into the importance of first loving yourself and then taking the time out to see beyond outward appearances to get to know those who are not like them. Kisha partnered with the WNBA team the Atlanta Dream and led their diversity and acceptance pillar through holding workshops for children and members of their corporate team. Her purpose is to create safe environments so that people can explore their truths.

Kayse Morris is a former eighth-grade English and language arts teacher who now helps teachers transition from being overwhelmed in life, to being thriving CEO Teachers. She is the host of a top-ranking business podcast called The Go-Getter's Podcast, where she helps entrepreneurs utilize business strategies that are proven to work. Kayse built a millionaire teacher mindset back in October of 2013, day by day and hour by hour. She was thinking "CEO Teacher" before that was even a thing. She now teaches other educators on how to build their own empires through her course "Transform Your Resources," and her membership group called "The CEO Teacher Academy." With nearly 100,000 followers on her social media channels, and thousands of testimonials, she's reached a point of happiness she never thought possible in life. You can find her and her daily motivational talks on Instagram @kaysemorris or get started building your future today at kaysemorris.com.

Bryce Sizemore began his teaching career in 2013 after receiving his M.Ed. from Southern Methodist University. During his time as a teacher, Bryce has taught kindergarten, first grade, and second grade in charter, public, and private schools. He began his business, The Teaching Texan, in 2014, during his second year of teaching, and has been sharing educational tips, strategies, and resources on his blog and in his TpT store. With the success of his business venture, Bryce expanded his resources to include both teacher and personal planners in the summer of 2016. In addition to his time spent in the classroom, blogging, and creating resources, Bryce has traveled across the country presenting on myriad educational development topics from literacy to math to hands-on science and beyond. More information about his professional development, resources, and planners can be found on his website at www.theteachingtexan.com.

Foreword

My friend Lisa Dunnigan asked me to spend a weekend in July 2019 listening to a group of educators, who were also entrepreneurs, tell their stories. My friendship with Lisa goes back 21 years. I understood her story and how and why she started a side hustle, but she felt that I needed to hear the other stories, too. Wow! What a weekend in New York with the 10 amazing educators who wrote this book. They shared with me their guide to helping teachers pursue their dreams outside of the classroom while maintaining presence in the classroom. They have centered themselves around people who "propel them to level-up."

These talented edupreneurs show us how they used problem solving and creativity to build high-demand, innovative products and services that complement their passion for teaching. They use creative problem solving to build a market that helps support their families' economic futures while improving their roles, networks, and competencies for teaching.

It may seem counterintuitive, but spending time working for yourself, on your own side hustle, makes you far more valuable in your full-time job. As a college business professor and business owner, I earn my living in five different ways: writing books, speaking, consulting, executive coaching, and teaching online courses. If one of those avenues goes away, I have enough diversification that I can focus on teaching instead of worrying about how I am going to pay my household expenses. As I listened to each of their stories that weekend, I found the answers to the following questions: What can you do? How much can you earn? What are the risks and rewards? Why develop entrepreneurial side ventures—even if you love your day job and have no intention of making a change?

Entrepreneurship is based on creating activities and implementing new ideas and concepts that are change-oriented. Each of the teachers embodies change for progress both individually and within the classroom. Their self-discipline, self-awareness, and understanding of their resources helps to propel them to achieve success in their own ways. Whether you work for yourself or for others, you'll need to find ways to diversify your income streams, your network, and learning. In most cases, your side venture may increase your status and marketability at work because of the new skills and competencies.

Competencies shared by the edupreneurs include the ability to operate actively and offer new activities to others, independence, and decisiveness while sharing knowledge with others on how to take risks, establish goals, design achievable plans of implementation, overcome difficulties, and solve complex problems. Edupreneurs need to become comfortable with the uncomfortable and learn adaptability, creative problem solving, communication, teamwork, and how to manage failure.

Each author has found ways to diversify their income streams, networks, and their love for life-long learning in order to become entrepreneurs. They are ambitious educators who take risks to empower teachers and others to discover their passions, talents, and skills on the side. Their handbook provides a guide for teachers who want to transform their ideas and passions outside of teaching into marketable skills and products.

—*Marilyn Carroll*

Marilyn Carroll, PhD, lives in Dallas, Texas. She is a writer, speaker, entrepreneur, and business professor. She is the author of several books including *Leap7: Launching Entrepreneurial Avenues of Possibilities*.

Preface

Everything in Your Career Has Prepared You for This Moment

No one will argue that the world of education has rapidly changed and evolved in the last 25 years, on so many levels. When many of us began teaching so many years ago, computers were brand new, desktops were the hot new device, laptops and cell phones were not even a thing, the internet was brand new, and email didn't exist. If anyone had told us then the word "edupreneur" would be a word in 2019, we wouldn't have believed them. For the purpose of this book, we define edupreneur as *an ambitious, risk-taking educator who empowers teachers to discover their passions, talents, and skills . . . and knows it's okay to make money doing it*. Not one of us started out as edupreneurs. We all began our professional journey as teachers, and we all work with teachers every day, just in different ways. While some of us are still full-time in the classroom with a part-time side hustle, some of us have turned our side hustle into a full-time hustle. Collectively, we have over 135 years of teaching experience bound within this book. We all have one love in common: teaching. While we love students, we love teachers, too. This book was written by teachers for teachers. In this book, we do not believe, nor are we saying, "leave teaching and make more money doing something else." We wrote this book to empower teachers who have a desire to discover their passion and make money doing it. Four out of five teachers in the United States have a second job, from working retail to airline customer service, babysitting, driving for Uber, or making and selling crafts to friends and family. Teachers find themselves taking on jobs outside the classroom to make ends meet. This is a handbook, a guide, written to honor and recognize that some educators have a desire to start their own business on the side, a "side hustle," but don't know where to begin or what to do next. They have an idea, a teaching degree, and a cell phone. Let us help you with the nuts and bolts of starting your own business.

Thanks to the internet and social media, more teachers have become empowered to make a global difference in the lives of teachers and students all over the world. Teachers feel more empowered than ever before to share their passion, be creative, and help make education better for everyone. However, most teachers like us got started with a college degree in education. Many teachers also have a master's degree in curriculum and instruction or instructional technology. A few teachers go on to pursue a doctorate in education or administration. However, most teachers do *not* have an MBA; teachers do not have formal training in business and marketing. Teachers know curriculum, not cash cows. Teachers know classroom management, not customer metrics. Teachers know math and phonics, not market segments. Teachers know verbs like *analyze, evaluate,* and *summarize,* not *monetize, strategize,* and *incentivize.* Teachers know acronyms like ZPD (Zone of Proximal Development), not FTZ (Free Trade Zone). And we're not saying we know all of the business terms even now, but we will say that, for the most part, we are all each completely self-taught when it comes to the business side of our own edupreneur side hustles.

Everyone reading this book is somewhere on the side hustle continuum. You've probably read memes on social media that say "Comparison is the thief of joy" or "Don't compare someone else's Chapter 20 to your Chapter 1." Some of you already have a business, some of you have a business name and a business email, and some of you are incorporated, which means your business name has an Inc. or LLC at the end of it. Some of you make and sell products on Teachers Pay Teachers, and most of you are considering or wondering whether you could be successful making and selling products in an online digital marketplace. Some of you may be reading this book because you think you'd like to make a go of doing professional development or professional coaching beyond your school, either through face-to-face or online teaching or through coaching using Facebook or course-building sites. Wherever you are in your professional journey, everything you've done in your career, every training, every conference, every hard lesson, has undoubtedly, collectively, prepared you for this moment, for the moment you have decided to enter the free market of capitalism, the American dream, of creating and owning your own business, to become your own boss. For every edupreneur author in this book, we each have a different level of educational experience, training, educational level, and position, and we each have a slightly different niche within educational side hustles. Up to this point, there have been no other books like this in the field of education, so we are beyond excited to share our edupreneurial advice, tips, and business strategies with you.

1

Getting to Know The Wright Stuff Chics

Lisa Dunnigan and Tosha Wright

Meet Lisa:

At 18, I had twin girls, Tosha and Elise. Even though I was a single mom, I was determined to get a college degree. While working two jobs the entire time, I was able to achieve that in four and a half years. Tosha and Elise's father was not in the picture very much, but our family was always there to help take care of them while I was working and attending classes. Ever since I was in first grade, I had wanted to be a teacher. I had an amazing student teacher. She mesmerized me, and she ignited a love for teaching in me. I was determined to be a successful teacher. My dad tried to talk me out of becoming a teacher; he said that I was not going to make any money. I told him that I was going to marry a rich man. Well, I married an educator! We had an awesome life and were able to give our girls an amazing life. We divorced after being married for 18 years. There are no regrets with my marriage and the life that we were able to have for Tosha and Elise. I taught seventh and fourth grade for seven years. God bless middle school teachers! Teaching fourth grade was my love for sure. I have been a school counselor, an assistant principal, and an elementary principal, and I have been a central office administrator over several federal programs for the last seven years. Having reached my 30-year mark, I will retire in February 2020 and will be able to focus on our brand and our non-profit, The Pink Santa Hat Movement, Inc. Being an educator has been one of the most rewarding aspects of my life. My desire is to continue to help other educators be successful in and out of the classroom.

Meet Tosha:

I never wanted to be a teacher, but isn't it funny how God works? I attended the college of my dreams (seriously my dream since I was a little girl) and was determined to be anything but a teacher. I changed my major continuously. When I entered college, my major was accounting. I took it in high school and loved it, but I quickly learned that it was not a good idea for me. After about two years of going back and forth, I finally started to research ways that I could possibly be a teacher (imagine that) and still graduate on time. I was able to change my major going into my junior year. My classes were interesting and applicable. Once I graduated in 2005, I enrolled in a two-year alternative program to receive teacher certification while I taught. I can honestly say that I was born to be an educator. It is ingrained in me and brings me more joy than frustration. I taught kindergarten and first grade, and it has been such a learning experience. I learned so many things about myself. Being in the classroom was fulfilling, but I felt like I needed to reach teachers on another level. I was a curriculum coordinator and now as a school leader, my heart is in the school and in working with students, their families, and teachers to help improve education. I tried to fight it many times and in many different ways, but I know I am where I am supposed to be.

I knew from the beginning that my teaching salary was not going to be enough to provide me with the things that I had grown accustomed to. Honestly, that was one of the reasons that I did not want to become a teacher. But I knew there were many things I could do to supplement my salary. Since my first teaching job, I always worked a part-time job. Whether it was tutoring, working at an after-school program, working in a clothing store (where I never actually earned a check because I bought so many clothes), or working for the Census, these side jobs allowed me to take trips, pay off debt, and just enjoy life. It is not my goal to quit my job because of our side hustle but to enhance my life and my family's life. I will tell you that it is very hard to balance it all—a full time job and being a wife, a mother, and a friend, and all while trying to stay healthy and take care of myself. My husband does more than his fair share at home, and he also does so much for our business—really anything that is asked of him. I know that I am doing exactly what I'm supposed to be doing in life right now. I'm so grateful that I didn't end up with what I thought I wanted.

Starting Our Brand

The Wright Stuff Chics, Inc., has opened many doors for our family. None of this would be possible without our loyal customers. We have some customers who bought our very first shirt and continue to buy our newest designs. Having a side hustle has been part of our family forever! Lisa always has to have one million balls in the air. That is how she functions, and Tosha got to watch all of it growing up, so it is also part of her DNA. Having a successful business is for sure not for the faint at heart, and it also takes lots of time, commitment, dedication, tears, and ups and downs. We started The Wright Stuff Chics, Inc., in December of 2016. Tosha's twin sister, Elise, started a faith-based t-shirt line when she was diagnosed with stage IV breast cancer. After seeing how successful Elise's business was, Lisa had an idea. We had previously run a very successful eBay shop with embroidery and gifts. We were a top seller store, but when Lisa got divorced, the business was sold. Lisa, Tosha, and Elise were on a three-way phone call where we bounced around several ideas and finally decided to get some cute and trendy teacher t-shirt designs made. We went back and forth on a name. Tosha had done birthday chalkboards, vinyl decals, and ornaments called The Wright Vinyl & Chalkboards. Elise actually came up with our name: The Wright Stuff. Using Tosha's last name was an easy way to tie this in as a family business. We later had to add Chics because the Wright Stuff was taken. Our very first design was Queen of the Classroom, and it has been a very successful design that we have revamped a couple of times. We even have a Spanish version now! Even though Tosha lived in Pennsylvania, we decided to have the business in Georgia because we have more family members who could help us here. We started out just shipping from our dining room. We did this for over a year. We had designs in three of the four bedrooms. Lisa's bedroom is where we packed the shirts, so we had the postage printer and all of the packing items there. All things Wright Stuff had taken over the entire house!

Once we knew that things were continuing to grow, we began to look at warehouse space. We needed a place to store the shirts and process orders. We ended up renting a storage-type unit near Lisa's house. We were there for about a year before we found a much bigger space that we were able to design ourselves. Our current warehouse has a retail space up front, where we can host pop-up shops as well as sell to customers at special events. In the back is where the magic happens. We store our tees, mugs, and shipping materials, and we package and label each order by hand. We have a full-time office manager and several part-time employees who help us to keep everything going in the right direction.

Refining Our Processes

During our first big after-Christmas sale, we received over 1,000 orders. Tosha and her family had to go back home after visiting during the holidays. Lisa also had a lot going on, as her doctor found a polyp on her intestines that needed to be removed. The doctor took out several inches of her colon, so she could not do any heavy lifting. Also, during this time we did various designs using heat transfer vinyl. We had over 150 shirts to weed before they could get heat pressed. If you have ever done this, then you know how labor-intensive it is. During the process of printing out those shirts, Lisa decided that vinyl did not need to be part of our brand. It does not hold up, and screen printing is way more durable and long lasting. Also during this time, we had one screen printer who printed all our shirts. Lisa called him to let him know that we had gotten over 1,000 orders. The first words out of his mouth were that it would take three weeks to print all the shirts because there were several different designs. Three weeks was way too long to make people wait for a design. We decided to contact another printer as well, and we were able to get out all of the designs within two weeks. That was the start of something big in our lives.

After the sale, we realized we needed help—and not just from other family. We needed to invest in someone working for us part-time to fill orders, handle customer questions and emails, and just in general help with fulfillment. We also decided that we needed to get our name out there. If you look on social media, you will see that there are at least a dozen online stores that sell teacher tees. We knew we needed help with branding and exposure, so we put out an ad for a social media manager to help us become successful with our teacher tee business. We wanted someone who could run our social media accounts since we both were working full-time jobs and did not have the time and energy to devote to making posts. We interviewed several people via phone and their online portfolios. Our amazing social media manager, Cynthia of Social One Marketing, has grown our business tremendously. Recently, we started working with an ad specialist, Greg, who has done a great job getting our ad game on. He has already given us an awesome strategy to turn into a multi-million-dollar company.

Find the (W)Right People

We have also opened many doors for those who work with us. It is important to find your people when it comes to starting a business. Find people who are loyal to you and your brand. We had no idea that our business would take off like it did. It was rough in the beginning because we had so many ideas but just the two of us to implement them. We have grown our business to two full-time employees and five part-time employees. Because Lisa and Tosha have always been supervisors on their jobs, the dynamics of managing adults has been the same even in our own business. We attribute our success to having great workers who always do their best to get the job done. Of course, there have been ups and downs in the last three years, but overall we have had great success.

> It is important to find your people when it comes to starting a business. Find people who are loyal to you and your brand.

What we do might seem easy, but there is so much that goes into making a business successful. We could have given up long ago, especially when things did not go our way. We have incurred many obstacles that could have taken us out, but we continued to press on. We vend for various events around the country

almost every weekend throughout the year. The worst experience we have had so far is when we had a driver who left from
Atlanta and would head to the weekend destination a couple of
days before the Saturday event. During this particular instance,
the driver left on Wednesday and was headed to Connecticut,
or so we thought . . . he ended up going to Arkansas, which
was totally the wrong direction. Once he figured it out, he was
24 hours away from the correct location. The only thing for him
to do was find the closest FedEx and ship the crucial items that
we needed. Lisa was distraught because experience had told her
that this was going to be an expensive mistake. The packages
arrived in Connecticut for the show and everything worked out
for the weekend. A week later we received the bill—over $10,000
in shipping costs. This experience taught us to make sure that the
directions are printed out and that our travel person goes over
the exact location with the driver before leaving our shop.

Although we have amazing employees who work hard daily
helping our business thrive, we have learned the hard way that
you cannot expect *you* from people.
Let that sink in and really think about
what that means. Yes, we employ
others and trust that they will meet
their job duties and expectations. But
at the same time, as an owner of a
company, you are way more invested

> Although we have amazing employees who work hard daily helping our business thrive, we have learned the hard way that you cannot expect *you* from people.

than they will ever be. That is a hard lesson. We trusted people
who said they could help grow our business but really just
wanted to get paid and not show any results. Some people do
not want to see you succeed. Over the years, this has been one of
the hardest lessons to learn in our business.

Oh, Inventory

Getting our inventory right has been one of the biggest
obstacles, especially when we have sales. We deal with three to

four different screen-printing companies at all times because we try our best to get out the orders within 15 days. This past summer, we had a grab bag sale where the customers were able to choose the three designs that they wanted. This was a major issue because our normal inventory could not be used. We tried our best to guess how many we needed. That was a disaster, to say the least. As we were packaging the orders, we would get down to the last two orders and need more shirts. Needless to say, the grab bag sales will never happen again. Many things in business are trial and error. Neither Tosha nor Lisa have business backgrounds. In the coming months, we are going to work with some inventory experts and get suggestions on what they think we should do. The good news is that we have lots of data that we can use in our Shopify history. We are going to improve our system. Amazon Prime's two-day shipping has spoiled people! They want their items within two to three days. That is not possible for us. Hopefully one day we will be able to do it. Getting the basics of the business down is something we continue to strive for daily. We have so many popular designs that narrowing them down is a daunting task. There are some designs we have tried to stop producing, but then a teacher will post themselves in the design and we get emails wanting to purchase the design. It is hard to juggle all the moving parts. This is probably one of our biggest issues in our business. On one hand, we do not want a lot of inventory in the warehouse but on the other hand, not having the shirts to fill orders is a big issue as well. We are trying to find a logistics and fulfillment person who can help us with this major issue.

Did Someone Say Teachers Love Rae Dunn Mugs?

This might sound crazy, but God always sends these ideas to Lisa. One of her ideas was to create a "Teach Your Heart Out" mug with Rae Dunn. After some research, Lisa was able to speak to someone at the company. Within weeks, the sample was ordered. We knew that they entire process would take 120 days because the mugs are made in a factory in China. We decided that we would do a presale on the mugs and would make sure that everyone knew that the mugs would take time to be made. We knew that teachers loved Rae Dunn, but we had no idea that the mug was going to be so popular. We received so many emails and direct messages asking us whether the mugs were authentic Rae Dunn mugs. Rae Dunn even posted "real" on one of our posts. This totally helped to validate that the mug was real. We learned so much during this process. For the next Rae Dunn order, we will be getting a fulfillment company to mail out all of the orders for us. It took us a month to get the thousands of orders sent out. Also, it took a little while to get the shipping process perfected. Our fulfillment manager watched a ton of YouTube videos, and we visited FedEx and UPS to garner advice on how to best ship the mugs. We did finally master getting them to show up unbroken. The next order will be much smoother.

Teach Your Heart Out Conferences

Over the last 29 years, Lisa has attended thousands of conferences. So many years ago, she put hosting an engaging and inspirational teacher conference on her bucket list. She had hosted several successful church conferences and knew that hosting a teacher conference could be just as successful. The goal of the teacher conference was to ensure that all participants walked away with strategies that could be easily implemented in the classroom, all while inspiring educators to continue to give 110% in the classroom. Our kids deserve only the best, and educators have a huge responsibility to the kids they teach. Our first conference completely sold out after we added Gerry Brooks to the lineup. Gerry has since been at every conference as a keynote speaker. After the first conference, we changed the name from

The Wright Stuff Chics, Inc., Conference to Teach Your Heart Out (TYHO). We also contacted Michelle Griffo of Target Teachers and Apples and ABC's to help us with getting our TYHO speakers. The conferences have been very well-received, and we hope to continue to build a successful conference that has a vast impact on classrooms all over the world. Recently, we took TYHO on a cruise ship. We had our classes right on the ship, and we also visited a local school in the Bahamas, which totally warmed the hearts of the educators who were in attendance. It was great to see how other countries view and teach the curriculum. Our next cruise will set sail to the Western Caribbean. With TYHO, we have the same goals, but our name is a reminder to each and every person who attends to Teach Your Heart Out always.

The Pink Santa Hat Movement

In 2017, Elise Dunnigan Bethel, Lisa's daughter and Tosha's twin sister, was diagnosed with stage IV metastatic breast cancer. Elise had started a faith-based tee line, and this helped her to remain positive and upbeat during her three-year illness. The year before she passed away, she encouraged us to start a non-profit. She even came up with the name: The Pink Santa Hat Movement. After discussing what we would do in the non-profit, we agreed that we wanted to somehow bring inspiration and encouragement to people who were battling breast cancer. We wanted it to be an easy fit in our brand, so we decided to solely focus on educators who are battling breast cancer. The first year we chose 10 women to whom we sent Christmas care packages. It was so much fun to shop for women who were going through treatment. Shipping out those packages brought a lot of joy to all three of us. We received some of the sweetest notes from the ladies who received a care package. The next year, we decided to choose eight women to bring to Atlanta, Georgia, for a weekend of pampering and inspiration. We provided them with a shopping trip, makeover, and photo shoot. The night was so amazing, and seeing the women being able to bond and talk about their treatments and life with cancer was remarkable. In January, we decided to send care packages throughout the year that would provide some inspiration to them. We hope to be able to grow our non-profit into something nationally. We know that over 268,000 women and men are diagnosed with breast cancer each year. We also want to bring some joy to educators who are having to deal with this dreadful disease that affects the entire family.

Pause and Reflect

What is your game plan for your business?
How much money are you going to need to start your business?
What problem will your product solve, or what benefit will it offer?
Who is your biggest competitor, and what sets you apart from them?

Don'ts of Starting a Side Hustle

- ◆ Do not measure your success based on what you see on social media. There is no way to know all the ins and outs of a business by what you see on social media.
- ◆ Find a group of people whom you can bounce ideas off of.
- ◆ Dream big! Lisa is the dreamer in our partnership. She always comes up with ideas that are out of the box. Many of the ideas that she has come up with have been very successful. Sometimes Tosha has to rein her back into reality.
- ◆ Don't overshare on social media. It is important to build relationships with your customers, but it's not necessary to share every single thing that happens.
- ◆ Don't try to start out too big. Find your niche and get all the steps worked out in your business before you try to grow quickly.

♦ We know in teaching that collaboration and borrowing ideas is an acceptable process, but in business it is not good to borrow someone else's ideas. We have had to get our lawyer to send lots of cease and desist letters. Most of the time our designs are stolen, and the person uses vinyl to remake them. It is not flattering that someone takes our ideas. It is an unacceptable practice that needs to stop.

♦ If you make clothing, find yourself a reliable screen printer. Your customers will be happy that you used a screen printer rather than vinyl.

Do's of Starting a Side Hustle

♦ Do make sure that you have done your research before you decide what product you want to market.

♦ Do think of the name you want for your business and ensure that no one else has the name. Check with your local courthouse to determine whether the name is already registered to another business.

♦ Do be original! Imitation is *not* the biggest form of flattery!

♦ Do start small! There is no way to grow overnight.

♦ Do ask for help! Invest in a business coach.

♦ Do have some core beliefs about your business. One of our main ones is that we believe in always giving back to our customers. We try to always have giveaways and great sales. Our goal is to have every teacher know about The Wright Stuff Chics, Inc.

♦ Find yourself a reliable accountant and lawyer. This is especially important if you have contracts in your business.

Tosha and Lisa know that there are a ton of companies that make graphic tees for educators. But what sets The Wright Stuff Chics, Inc., apart is the positive impact that we are having on education. One of our core beliefs is to always give back. We don't always turn a huge profit on everything that we do, and we like it like that because at the end of the day we want people to say that we are making an impact on the world of education. Also, we know that we are living out the purpose that God has set for us, and we know that we have something special going on in the world of education. We are the magic in The Wright Stuff Chics, Inc.

2

Too Legit to Quit

Hello Business Basics

Jen Jones

Literacy Is and Has Always Been My Passion

As I begin my 26th year in education, I reflect back on my first year of teaching. I was hired at an elementary school after the school year had started in September. My interview was on a Wednesday, I was hired on Thursday, and I had three short days to get my classroom ready for my new group of third graders, all who were coming out of other overcrowded classes. Parents were either going to be happy their children got moved or mad they got moved. It turned out to be a good year. I didn't get fired. I learned a ton, both about teaching students and about teaching parents. I stayed too late, too often, but mostly, I learned that a teacher's job is never done. After three years, I began teaching Reading Recovery, an intensive training that has, thus far, taught me the most about teaching reading of any training or schooling I've done since. In the last 25 years, I have taught in California, Florida, and North Carolina. Teaching at PK Yonge Developmental Research School at the University of Florida prepared me for having teacher visitors from around North

Central Florida observe in my classroom almost every week. This became a regular practice that kept my teaching top notch and quickly built my confidence. When you and your students are doing great things in the classroom, you welcome visitors because you don't have anything to hide.

When I finished my master's in reading education in 2009, it was right about the time I was asked to open a brand new elementary school in a very large district in North Carolina. This would be my first year "out" of the classroom, but still working in the school building supporting teachers in the classroom and co-teaching alongside them. One of the most effective ways to serve the largest number of students and to increase literacy achievement is to co-teach with teachers inside their classrooms. By elevating the level of instruction and pedagogy of the teacher, you elevate the teaching and learning of everyone in the room, including students. (You can read more about the most effective methods for student-centered, literature-based literacy instruction in my professional book, *Get Your Lit Together*.) As the response to intervention coordinator, I developed the school's literacy intervention protocols, created the forms, and trained each grade level in the intervention and progress monitoring process. For three years, I served as the school improvement chair and literacy committee chair, working with my committee to develop a Literacy Classroom Walkthrough Form with Look-Fors and Listen-Fors based on our school's literacy Key Processes and Action Steps. All of my teaching experience and literacy leadership roles are the content foundations of Hello Literacy, Inc., my business. Literacy is and has always been my passion; it began as a side hustle and has now become my full-time hustle.

In this chapter, I will be sharing four aspects of starting a side hustle with you:

1. Why your positive presence is integral in the school community and is an important professional prerequisite to your side hustle;

2. What you must do to gain credibility and trust with potential customers;
3. Essential considerations for branding, naming, legalizing, and marketing your business; and
4. How to stay relevant and real in a world where transparency and authenticity are everything. I will also share with you the number one business secret most of your competitors don't know.

As you're reading, you might get the urge to put this book down in the middle of the chapter and get started on many of the strategies I mention. Please don't; read this entire chapter all the way to the end before doing anything. Don't start a blog, check domain names, or open a Teachers Pay Teachers (TpT) store. Trust me. If you want to annotate in the margins or make a list, that is fine, you know that's what engaged readers do.

Establishing Yourself as a Credible Expert

The more involved you are in your school community, the more you are prepared to run your own business and communicate with people, especially with educators. People skills are essential in any business. People skills are soft skills like communication, problem-solving, conflict resolution, initiative, and critical thinking. Twenty-five years of teaching and literacy leadership experience provided me with a hotbed of rich knowledge and experiences, as well as information and content to share with the world. In my position, I was able to get in and out of a lot of classrooms frequently. I was able to see and hear the amazing teaching and learning that was happening inside the classrooms and see the visual evidence of this learning displayed in the school hallways. These experiences led me to begin blogging in 2009. I blogged about the literacy best practices I was seeing, hearing, and a part of at my school.

I started my blog and called it Hello Literacy, with a tagline and mission of "Growing readers one best practice at a time." I began to blog consistently about best practices, resources, routines, texts, and reading comprehension skills and strategies, as well as writing, grammar and conventions, vocabulary, fluency, phonics, and phonemic awareness. I even blogged about digital literacy, along with other soft skills of 21st-century learning. I mention all the topics I covered to demonstrate what became my core values and passion. You'll want to draw on your areas of strength for idea generation.

If you have any desire to start a side hustle, you have a desire to creatively share your knowledge and talents with other teachers. Starting a blog may be one of the first business practices you will consistently put into place. No longer will you be a digital consumer. You will be making your mark on education as a whole, a space that is larger than you, your class, your school, or your district. Before you can take from teacher professionals, you must first give freely to the teacher professionals who will eventually become your target customers, those teachers who will eventually buy from you. Your blog (or website hosts that have a built-in blog feature) is where you'll put your free content and knowledge with no strings attached. It will be a landing spot where others can decide a) whether you know what you're talking about and b) whether they want to buy your product or service.

A blog is time-consuming. It's slow and steady. But the more you consistently add to it, the more you build trust with your audience and give them opportunity after opportunity to build long-term confidence in you. You will want to be cognizant not to make every blog post about "go buy this thing I made" or "go sign up for my this I created" or "do all these things to get this free thing." Your blog should be meaty with good-quality, original content shared freely ... *that* will build more trust than anything else. It doesn't matter how knowledgeable or credible you think you are. That is for others to decide from reading your blog.

> It doesn't matter how knowledgeable or credible you think you are. That is for others to decide from reading your blog.

If right now you're thinking, "why should I spend time writing blog posts that don't earn me any money when I could be making a product or course with a price tag?", think of it as an investment in your business. For many young teachers, Instagram and Facebook have become the new blogging. Platforms with shorter feed captions and video stories have replaced longer, more traditional blog posts. Until you write a book of your own, you'll want to put your original, quality content (ideas and opinions in your niche) out there somewhere consistently for others to find, read, and learn from. In my opinion, the advantage of writing on a blog vs. posting on Instagram or Facebook is that your content is Google searchable. In my opinion, when it comes to getting found or discovered as an expert in your niche, Google is key because more teachers will do an information search on Google than a hashtag search on social media.

Regarding protecting your ideas you blog about, that is called copyright, and you own them. The original ideas you write about, share with the world, and express in your own unique way are your intellectual property (IP). Simply by publishing your ideas (with a date and time stamp) on your blog to the web, you hold the copyright to the original content contained in the blog post. If you are sharing someone else's idea, you should seek their permission to do so on your blog. Otherwise, you run the risk of leading your blog readers to believe that it's your original content when it's not—and that is misleading and shady. Those are adjectives that you do not want associated with you or your brand.

Finding Your Passion Means Finding Your Niche

Before you decide to start a side hustle—or tweak an existing side hustle that might be lacking a clear purpose, focus, plan, and long-term goals—you need to stop and reflect on your professional philosophy, your teaching beliefs, and your passion. The common denominator of your professional philosophy, your teaching beliefs, and your passion will be your niche, your wheelhouse. It will become what you are known for, what others seek from you, and what will keep you in your professional lane when other educational and social fads and influences for teachers try to pull you away and distract you from your niche.

> If you are growing a side hustle into a business, you do not want to be general. You want to be specific and have a specialized niche, product, and/or service that is unique to you and your brand.

If you are growing a side hustle into a business, you do not want to be general. You want to be specific and have a specialized niche, product, and/or service that is unique to you and your brand. It should be something that others can easily identify or something they see or hear in the world that makes them think of you if they notice it when you're not around. I get direct messages from teachers daily sending me pictures of HELLO signs, libraries, pictures of children reading, lip gloss, tacos, and anything with flowers on it. These are items and artifacts associated with Hello Literacy and my personality, out in the world. My brand.

Pause and Reflect

To recap and reflect, you'll want to stop, think, and write down on paper the answers to the following questions:

What is my professional philosophy?
(*A format statement or bulleted list*)
What are my teaching beliefs?
(*Your educational opinions*)
What in education (teaching and learning) am I most passionate about?
(*Beliefs you stand up for, fight for, and vocalize publicly*)
What is the common denominator of my philosophy, beliefs, and passion?

(What your philosophy, beliefs, and passion have in common will be your niche)
What product and/or service will I provide to other teachers in my niche?
(The visible, marketable resources and/services you will create, market, and sell)

So, starting a blog is now on your to-do list. But, if you truly want to set yourself apart, it's not enough to be an expert online. Your online customers want to know that you have the professional trust and respect of the teachers in your own building. Potential customers want to know that the teachers you work with on a daily basis also think of you as a respected colleague, and it may not seem necessary, but it's really about character and integrity, so if you are a respected teacher in your real-life school community, then you won't have anything to worry about.

Locking Down Your Brand

Once you've found your niche, you'll want to build your brand by first deciding on a catchy name for your business. It could simply be your name, or it could be a memorable phrase, like Hello Literacy, Easy Teaching Tools, or The Teaching Texan. Check out the business names of some of the co-authors of this book. This might seem like an easy and fun step, but there are a few things to consider. The brainstorming process is rather fun. You'll throw hundreds of names out there. You'll sleep on them, and you'll invest time and creative energy into picking just the right name. You'll narrow it down to one or two that you really love—they will be so uniquely "you" that you'll say to yourself, "this is so unique to me, no one else could possibly have this!" Then you'll discover it's already taken. And all the days and hours you worked so hard to find a name just slipped through your fingers. So you will go back to the drawing board, a bit less enthusiastic than you were at first. This energy pump and drain is normal. It will happen a lot during the journey of your business. You will learn more from your mistakes and failures than from your successes. To ensure that no one else has the business name that you want to use, I recommend that you check your ideas in the following places. If they all check out and are available, you're good to go:

TESS Trademark Database

This database is at the U.S. Patent and Trademark Office (USPTO) website. When you go to www.uspto.gov, select "Trademarks" and scroll down to "Search TESS," select "Basic Word Mark Search," and enter the business name you want to use in the search term box. Let's say you are interested in branding the name The Taco Teacher. You would enter just the words: "The Taco Teacher" and click "Submit Query." Your green light is when it says "No TESS records were found to match the criteria of your query." If you type in "Hello Literacy" in the search term box, or even the Nike phrase "Just Do It," you'll see they are *live* registered trademarks. That means they are taken. You'll definitely want to trademark your business name so it's *yours*. The process to trademark is not fast; in fact, it takes about 9 to 12 months from start to finish. I speak from experience when I say *do not* use popular legal websites to do this for you. I did and my trademark application was rejected, and I had to hire an attorney to "clean it up" and finally get it approved. Find an IP attorney in your town and hire them from the beginning for this process. In general, trademarking your business name will cost around $750 to $1,000 including USPTO trademark fees and attorney fees, but it will be well worth it in the end. This process, though, is not for the font style, word size/placement, image, or logo associated with your brand; it is only for the words themselves.

Blog Name and Address

If you haven't actually started your blog yet, you'll want to now check that no one else has a blog with the same name. It is very possible that someone does have the URL of thetacoteacher dot blogspot dot com. If that is the case, you can do a few things. You can start over and find another name. You can reach out to the blog owner and ask them if they would be willing to transfer it to you. Or, you can use a different blog platform like Weebly, Wix, or WordPress. You'll want to research the price, inclusions, and ease of use when deciding on your blog hosting site.

Domain Name

You will also want to purchase the domain name thetacoteacher. com. You can check the availability of domain names by searching sites like godaddy.com. If it's available, it will say something like "thetacoteacher.com is available" and will prompt you to add it to your cart. If dot org and dot net are also available, it will prompt you to purchase them as well. Dot com is so common, but buying the others is your choice. The advantage to buying your business domain name's dot net and dot org addresses is that you capture all the people looking for your site but not correctly typing it into the URL bar. Once your blog (or website) is up and running, you can forward anyone from the dot net and dot org search over to your dot com site. I strongly suggest you purchase your domain name now, even if you don't use it for a couple of years. At least you own it. It's a cheap investment for an online presence that is your unique brand. If you are Nike, you want everyone to find you at nike.com.

Email Address

Creating an email account will be essential. Again, you'll want to make it intuitive for your customers or potential customers to get in touch with you, so your next move should be seeing whether thetacoteacher@gmail.com is available. If it's not available, you can try other close addresses, like tacoteacher@gmail. com. If those are not available, and you own your domain name, you can purchase an email suite with your domain name. That gets you "info@thetacoteacher.com," "contact@thetacoteacher. com," or "[yourname]@thetacoteacher.com." That is actually a smart business move because (and this is a business tangent) if you ever want to create custom brand GIFs that appear in Instagram stories, you need to create a GIPHY account using an email address like [yourname]@[yourdomainname].com. Gmail and Yahoo! email accounts are not accepted. GIPHY wants to know that you are a legit brand or business.

Banking Accounts

This step may come later for you, depending on how much money you make initially and how much you make with each growing year of your business. Chances are you'll be collecting money through bank transfers if you have a TpT store or directly through your website. In this case, you'll have to link a business checking account to a PayPal account of the same name through your website. I host my website through Wix.com, which has a Store feature for hard goods like my Hello Literacy merchandise and my events, like my #HelloLitCon events. At check-out, teachers can use PayPal or their credit card to pay for their purchases. If you have a personal PayPal account and a personal checking account at the bank, yet aren't sure when to open a business checking account and a business PayPal account, here's what I was told from two different sources: When you begin to earn between $20K and $30K a year from your side hustle, you should apply for an LLC or S-Corp. You'll want to hire an accountant at this point. Then you can take their advice into account as to which one is best for you, since accountants are much more familiar with the tax laws in your state. Some accountants and all IP attorneys can form a business entity for you, making your business legal in the eyes of the government. In that process, you'll be assigned a federal tax ID number, which is what is needed to create a business bank checking account as well as a business PayPal account that is linked to your business bank checking account. A large portion of my business is providing professional development to schools and districts that individually contract with me; 95% of those schools and districts want to pay me with a school or district check or purchase order, so I must first create an invoice for them, and they generate a check to pay the invoice. Some districts will ask for a W-9, which I will submit. Checks deposited into your business banking checking account must be made out to your business name—for example, the checks must be made out to Hello Literacy, Inc. (my business is an S-Corp), so I always include this direction at the bottom of my invoice. If your business is in need of generating invoices because your customer is a principal or a school that wants to pay using a purchase order, you can use the invoicing services of PayPal (or Stripe, or whatever you use to collect money online), which charges a service fee. Or you can create your own in PowerPoint like I do (no fee). You can also create your own from a free online template.

Social Media Handles

For brand consistency, you'll want to continue the "brand lock down" by using @thetacoteacher to start a Facebook page. "Page" is the term for a Facebook business page. You must have a personal Facebook account before you can create a Facebook business page. Next, you'll check Twitter and create an account for @thetacoteacher on Twitter. If you're thinking "I don't use Twitter" or "Why should I have a Twitter account?", then you're not thinking like an edupreneur. You might not use Twitter or know how to use Twitter for your potential customers, but they do and are looking to tag you on social media. You'll create an Instagram account and a Pinterest account as well. Those are the four most popular social media platforms used by teachers for both personal and educational use.

Social media is also the place where your customers will share your products and services on their social media pages and tag you. If you create hashtags that are unique to you, your customers will also use your hashtags in their posts and stories. For example, hashtags that are unique to my brand are #bookpusher, #jenjonessaidso, #everydayislibraryday, #getyourlittogether, #helloliteracy, and #hellolitcon. When your customers post, repost, and share on social media and tag you or follow your hashtags, their social media followers find you as well. Using hashtags in your posts helps your feed appear organically on the Instagram Explore Page, where you're seen by fresh new eyes and potential customers.

Colors, Clipart, and Commercial Use

Now that your business name is protected and locked down in all the right places, you'll decide on icons (if any) and will create a brand logo. Maybe it's an apple, a penguin, or a test tube; that's all up to you. Deciding on an icon is one thing, but finding an icon is another. There are edupreneur-friendly sellers on TpT. Some of my favorite TpT clip artists that are edupreneur friendly are Creating4theclassroom, Kate Hadsfield, Creative Clips, Melonheadz, and Zip-A-Dee-Doo-Dah. These are clip artists who will let you use their clipart commercially. Some Etsy sellers are commercial friendly too. When you find clipart you like, you should ask them, "Can I use this clipart in my business logo?" They may articulate whether clipart can be used for personal or commercial use. Personal use refers to using their work in ways that do not gain a profit. Commercial use means you have permission to use what you purchase in your products and services for which you charge money and earn a profit. Another website that allows for commercial use is flaticon.com. If you create an account and pay for commercial use of their icons, it contains thousands of clipart logos available for use in your business. Websites and apps that allow for free commercial use of photographs and stock images are Pexels, Unsplash, Pixabay, and Morguefile.

Next, you'll select colors that match your brand. You may want to do a little bit of color research. When it comes to marketing psychology, there's a lot of information out about colors and their emotional effect on consumers. For example, red is a power color, and a lot of big brands use it in their logo: Target, YouTube, CNN, Netflix, Coca-Cola, Lego, and Kellogg's. I'm not saying make a red logo; I'm saying do your homework. You'll want to choose logos and designs unique to your brand name and brand image. My icon or logo is a flower bunch, as my mission is to "grow" readers one best practice at a time. I purchased my brand clipart from a website called creativemarket.com and paid for commercial use of the clipart.

Social Media Is the New Yellow Pages

Although marketing your business on social media is covered elsewhere in this book, I must wrap up this chapter by saying that social media is the new Yellow Pages. If you're old enough to know what the Yellow Pages are, then you'll probably want to pay attention to how much your social media use for business could significantly and positively impact your business. You may or may not be among the people who say "I'm not good with technology" or "I don't know how to do that stuff." If you are a millennial or born after 1985, social media is probably second nature to you. My advice is this: Learn how to use social media because social media is free advertising. Social media is where your customers are. Post nuggets about your niche; give ideas away for free. Create short, original, helpful, quality posts for social media and post consistently. Consistency is key. Whether you post once a day or three times a day, if you don't show up for your audience, they won't show up for you. That being said, make your posts relevant, helpful, and high quality, with original content aligned to your business. Don't fall into the trap of using Instagram like a personal Facebook, where post after post says "this is what is what I'm doing, this is where I'm going, this is my cute family, this is me on vacation, this is me getting a haircut." Remember you are using social media to promote your business by showcasing your products and services in action. So, you might be asking, "Should I have a personal Instagram and a business Instagram?" The answer is yes. In the case of my Instagram account, I create one personal post for every nine literacy posts on my feed. Think of Instagram Story as the behind-the-scenes of your feed, a place where you can video explain yourself and your business. Avoid posting giveaways. While this may get you some new followers at first, it makes your tried and true followers annoyed. In fact, I stopped doing them completely in the spring of this year because teachers are tired of having to like, comment, tag friends, and follow umpteen accounts for an iPad or an Amazon gift card. In addition, the followers you gain from a giveaway are not the type of teachers who authentically find you and choose to purposely follow you.

> Having an edupreneur side hustle is not just about creating something that people want and that you provide overnight. It's an ongoing process of brainstorming, branding, creating, marketing, posting, promoting, building, maintaining customer satisfaction, designing, and so much more.

Having an edupreneur side hustle is not just about creating something that people want and that you provide overnight. It's an ongoing process of brainstorming, branding, creating, marketing, posting, promoting, building, maintaining customer satisfaction (which could be an entire other book), designing, and so much more. All of that takes time to develop and refine. One last piece of advice that I want to leave you with is to find other like-minded people to ask for help, to cry to when things aren't going well, and to celebrate wins with when things do go well. Let them be your support system that you can rely on and trust to support you, inspire you, motivate you, and tell you the truth about your business, your professionalism, and your contribution to education.

3

The Great Balancing Act

Fitting It All In

Bryce Sizemore

"Hold on, this will just take me a minute." I don't know how many times I've uttered that statement to my husband, to a friend, or to a coworker. Y'all, if I can be completely honest with you for just one moment—and isn't that what we're here for?—*it never takes just a minute*. That social media post, edit to your blog, or email response to a customer is inevitably going to take more time than you initially think. And to be fair, you should be giving each aspect of your business and life the necessary time to do it correctly.

As a true southerner (hence my use of "y'all"), I should back up for a moment to allow for a more proper introduction. I'm Bryce Sizemore, the man behind The Teaching Texan blog, Teachers Pay Teachers (TpT) resource creation, professional development speaking, planners, and t-shirts. I have been a substitute teacher and have taught kindergarten, first grade, and second grade in public, charter, and private schools during my seven years as an educator. My home in Dallas, Texas, always seems to be bustling with all that's going on with my business ventures, my husband Dustin's career in real-estate development, our son Ace, and our two dogs Peatree and Aspen. If

I don't get my fix of working with kiddos during the day, I'm sure to get my fill during the several evenings a week that I coach competitive cheerleading for Spirit of Texas.

Sounds like a lot, doesn't it? Since we're great friends now, and since we're being completely honest with each other, I'll share with you that it is. The days are long, and I drink more than my fair share of coffee. But I've gained a lot of knowledge along my journey and have found ways to schedule my time so that I can balance my personal time with family and friends while growing a successful business. My hope is to share that knowledge with you in this chapter, so you can manage all of the pieces of your life that are important to you and your business.

Whatever season you are currently in with your business, know that it is a journey, and wherever you are is completely fine. In fact,

> Whatever season you are currently in with your business, know that it is a journey, and wherever you are is completely fine.

you should be proud of what you've done! Even if your start is reading this book itself, you are already ahead of the people who have only thought about it but not yet acted. Personally, I didn't start off wearing all of the hats that I currently do as The Teaching Texan. But because of my journey, I have added responsibilities and ventures to my plate as I have learned and grown. I think it's vital you know that I got my start in this whole beautiful adventure by creating resources for my classroom at a charter school where we weren't supplied with a curriculum. As I scoured teaching blogs for new ideas, I came across some blogs posts referencing TpT. I thought to myself, "I have all of these resources I've created, and maybe I could do this, too."

Setting and Prioritizing Goals

In those early years, I began with offering a few sight word coloring pages, math facts fluency, and a few other random resources. I mention the word *random* because when I first got started, I really didn't have a vision of what I wanted to share with the education community or even where I wanted things to go. At that time, I didn't consider what I was doing as a business. But those thoughts quickly changed. Whether you've been on your venture for some time or are just starting out, my first piece of advice is to sit down and reflect on your goals. I'm a huge proponent of goal setting because when we have a roadmap, we know our goal destination. All of the roads may not be laid out for us to easily follow, and we may take a few unexpected pit stops for setbacks or new opportunities that arise, but we can at least create a framework based on the goals we have set. With that framework in mind, we can often avoid the detours that take time away from the work that will take our business to and beyond our dreams.

Here are a few simple goal-setting questions to get you started. I recommend writing down your answers, not only because it allows you to refer back to your thought process at a later point but also because of the power that putting things in writing has. Anytime I'm thinking about my goals, I like to start off by asking myself, "where am I now?" If we're going to run the marathon—*and let's do it together*—we have to know where our starting line is. It's probably important to mention here that you cannot compare your starting line to anyone else's. The next thing I want you to ask yourself is where you want to be in five years. I like to start off with a distant goal and then go back in and fill in the "baby-step goals" that will help me get there. What big milestone are you hoping for? What impact do you hope to have made? Now that you know where you are and where you want to be, ask yourself, "how will I get there?" This is how you set your smaller goals that will drive you towards that five-year dream. Start breaking it down. For example, if you want to create 30 new products over the next five years, your baby-step goal may be to create one product every two months. See how that already makes 30 products seem more manageable? Having your smaller goals figured out will pay dividends when you sit down to plan out your time—*see where we're heading?*

Pause and Reflect

Where are you now?
Where do you want to be in five years?
How will you get there?

There's one last thing before we discuss scheduling out our time. I have a question for you. Have you heard of the Pareto Principle? I first learned about this concept a few years back while I was preparing to present on time management at the annual TpT Conference. The Pareto Principle, also known as the 80/20 Rule, states that 80% of our results come from 20% of the work we put in. Seems so simple, right? The challenge here is trying to determine *which* 20% of our efforts are leading to the maximum results. Here's how I do it. Take your list of goals you wrote in the previous section (and if you happened to skip that step, go back and do it now so you can find your 20%). The math will work out differently depending on how many baby-step goals you have written down—that is, if you have 10 goals total, then 2 would fit into your schedule. So if you only had time in your schedule to complete 20% of your goals, which would be deemed most important? Circle them. This is your 20% that will be most valuable in the growth of your business. Will you spend time on the others? Of course you will, but now you know what you should value most when divvying up your time.

Setting a Schedule

Ready to schedule? I hope so. Now you know what your goals are, and which are most important. That is where we start. When I plan, I like to sit down with paper and pencil, you know, old-school style. I sit down with a large cup of coffee, and I break out my The Teaching Texan planner and a pack of my favorite pens and highlighters. I like to work on at least a month at a time. The first thing I do is block out times when I am not available to work because of other obligations such as a full-time job and appointments. Next up, I add on my non-negotiables. These are things like working out (for me), date night, and time with family. What we are essentially doing is finding which times you are *actually* available for your side hustle. Go ahead and highlight the hours that you are realistically able to devote to your business. Don't worry if it's only a few hours a week at this point; remember that giving any time at all to this dream on a consistent basis puts you light years ahead of people who are only dreaming.

> Remember that giving any time at all to this dream on a consistent basis puts you light years ahead of people who are only dreaming.

With your availability for the next month clearly shown, you can now start to plug in your baby steps to meet your goals for your side hustle. Now here's the thing: You may need to get a little ambitious with your time and put in the hours early in the morning before your day starts or later into the evening after your day has wound down. My sweet spot is to wake up around 4:30 or 5:00 AM and work a few hours before anyone else gets up. Is it easy? No. But I've learned my mind works best early in the morning, and the chance for interruptions is quite minimal. (It's no surprise I've worked on this chapter for you during many a 4:30 AM work session.) Whenever works for you, keep in mind that even a few hours each week is more than not working on your business at all! I bet you know what should get plugged into your schedule first at this point. If you're thinking it's the 20% of your goals that would be deemed most valuable, you're correct. Once you've allotted time for those, go in and schedule the tasks needed to complete your other goals.

This starts to take you into your weekly and daily planning. Keep a list of those small goals that will help you reach your bigger goals. Each day, I like to start by getting focused on a couple of specific tasks that, once finished, not only will make me feel accomplished but will also help me take another step towards my goal. Baby steps are where it's at, y'all! Again, I write these down because I want to be able to look back at my personal journey and see all of the progress I have made. It really pays off to have this on those days you are feeling discouraged or unmotivated.

Pause and Reflect

What are your non-negotiables?
How much time can you realistically devote to your business?

Staying Focused With Batching

So here we are: We've got our month planned out, we've scheduled our baby steps and projects throughout the week, and we have sat down each day with a couple of specific tasks to complete. Here's where I have to share my thoughts on email, bills, and all of the rest of those routine-type tasks. I can sum it up for you in one simple word. Batching. I used to try and respond to emails throughout the day as they came in because I was scared that if I didn't respond immediately, I might offend someone or miss an opportunity. In reality, I was spending far too much time opening and closing my email, taking my mind out of "focus mode," and overthinking responses. On this journey, I've learned that batching my work not only saves time but also helps keep the mind focused where it should be. So what exactly is batching? Batching is where you schedule similar tasks into the same time of day. For example, I now generally respond to emails twice a day—once in mid-morning and once in the evening (barring any time-sensitive projects). It helps me stay focused throughout the day. And once I'm in "email mode,"

I find I can respond much more quickly. Another tip for emails is to keep a file on your computer with responses to common questions. I've been asked more times than I can count about my advice on becoming a teacher in Texas. By having a thought-out response pre-typed, I can answer this question and build a relationship with a potential customer. More importantly I'm saving myself time from typing the same thing over and over.

Long story short, batching works for all sorts of tasks. You can batch podcast recording, product creation, editing, photo shoots of products, and more. Do yourself a huge favor and try it out!

It should come as no surprise that if we are maximizing our time with scheduling that relates to our goals, and with batching to improve productivity, then we may also at some point consider bringing in help. I wrestled with where in the chapter to share this with you, because this point in our journey is so different for each of us. My husband jumped in about two years into the journey to help out with some tasks, but I know we may not all be in the situation where a spouse can help out. Around year five is when I hired the first outside person to help with The Teaching Texan. She was and still is a very close friend, and I brought her on to help write my blog posts. It's been a great fit because she is so familiar with my voice as a teacher and blogger. I personally recommend finding someone you know to help out with your business for this reason if you can.

During year seven of the business venture, I decided it was time to bring on someone who could help take on even more of the routine-type business tasks. I hired a virtual assistant (VA) to help out with my emails, Pinterest, some social media, and search engine optimization for my website. This was a huge step for me, not only in terms of releasing some control of the business to someone else but also financially. I say this because I don't want you to feel pressure to bring someone in before you are ready. I look at it this way: If having a VA helps free up even two or three hours a week for me, imagine what I could do with that time. I could create a new product or work on a new email funnel. That's exactly what I've done with that time. I know my investment in a VA, which allows for even more productivity to occur, is a sound one.

Staying Focused on Social Media

Let's talk a moment about social media. How do you feel about sharing your business or journey with the world? I've got a love–hate relationship with the whole idea. Take a picture or a video and share it with an endless sea of eyes around the world? It can be a little unsettling and even daunting. But the impact of the connections you can form through the use of social media will pay spades in the growth of your business—that is, if you do it right. Since we're all about balancing our time, the first realization I want to help you come to is that you can't do it all. There are so many platforms that are available on which to share your products, journey, or whatever it is you choose to share. If you are attempting to be present on them all, you have already severely limited the amount of time you will have for all of the other important aspects of growing your business.

I played around with Twitter, Facebook, Instagram, and Pinterest until I found what worked for me and the people I wanted to have connect with my business. For me, Instagram was the clear winner. My brand and personality mesh with the focus on teaching and lifestyle shared primarily through images. Instagram was a game changer. And with scheduling services like Tailwind, it feels completely manageable. I dabble with Facebook, but I very quickly learned that Twitter was not for me. It was hard to take that step back because at conferences and everywhere I turned, I heard that "every educator should be on Twitter." At the end of the day I got to make that call, however, and Twitter just didn't feel right. I didn't see the return I needed to make it worth it. With a reduced social media load, I was already saving time.

Reduce, reuse, recycle. That is not just a mantra for helping our planet, but is also one for social media. If you want to save yourself time, stop feeling the need to post every single day. Reduce the quantity of your posts while increasing the quality. If your followers become accustomed to you posting every

> Reduce, reuse, recycle. That is not just a mantra for helping our planet, but is also one for social media.

other day or every few days rather than every day, you will still have great engagement with them, and they will continue to be a part of your growing community. Another thing to reduce is the amount of social media you are consuming yourself. Now I'll be the first to raise my hand that I have been caught on more than a couple of occasions just mindlessly scrolling through Facebook or Instagram. But if we want to maximize our time, we have to put our phones down. If you lack self-control around this like I do, there are several apps available on the market that will "lock" you out of social media on your phone for a given time. My favorite to date is an app called Flipd. I can still access phone calls or emails if needed, but all forms of social media are temporarily removed from my access so that I can focus on my goals. Another way to maximize your time regarding social media is to reuse and recycle your old content. You spent your valuable time curating those images or ideas; why not share them again? As we grow on whatever social media platform we may be using, we have new followers who have never seen that old content. I often pop in a new picture with a very similar caption around an idea, or I recycle a quote that previously resonated. Yes, we have to curate new content, but don't forget about the valuable things you have already shared!

Pause and Reflect

How can you reduce your social media load?
Which platform(s) might be the best for you and your business?

Partnerships and Collaborations

Now that you aren't trying to do *all the things* on social media and your following is growing on the platform that work best for you, you are likely going to start hearing from companies, authors, and other edupreneurs seeking partnerships and collaborations. How exciting! I remember getting my first request for a collaboration. A self-published author asked me to share her new book on my social media platforms. I was elated someone thought so highly of my brand to feel it was a good fit for her to share her product on my social media. Happily, I created my post and shared it out to my followers. Over the years, I have been blessed to partner with some amazing brands—Staples, Lakeshore Learning, and Carson Dellosa, to name a few. So how did I manage my time with all of the requests that were coming in?

I learned to say "no, thank you." When I first started out, I was excited to have someone reach out asking me to share about their book, product, or mission. During those days, I was so excited to even be thought of that I would quickly say yes to sharing things for free. I know that those humble beginnings helped to grow my social media presence to where it is today. But as my business grew, so did the number of requests for partnerships. I had to take a step back and realize that not every partnership benefitted or fit with my brand. When we share things for others, what we share should be a reflection of who we are and what our business stands for. At the end of the day, we have only a finite amount of time to work on our business, and it takes time to procure successful social media posts to partner and collaborate with others. It was hard to learn to say no, but I did and you will, too. In fact, in the spirit of being a teacher, I'll show you how "Thank you so much for considering me to share your wonderful book. I absolutely love how your book speaks to ____. The illustrations are absolutely breathtaking! My brand is all about engaging teaching strategies for K–2, sharing light-hearted humor, and inspiration. Therefore, I don't think that I'm the best fit to share your book, but I wish you continued success!" There, wasn't that easy? You've validated that the product you've been asked to share has value and shown you care for his/her success, and at the same time you've shown respect to yourself and your time.

Let's Put a Bow on It

There are a million and one things you'll do to grow your successful business—*and I know you can do it!* There will be days you feel totally overwhelmed, and I'm here to tell you that's okay. I have days like that, too. We all do. Keep your focus on your big goals and on the baby steps you will take to get there. Be gracious when scheduling your time. It's not a competition to see who can spend the most time on their side hustle. It's all about creating the life *you* want. Remember that it's okay to say no. We're all human and we can't do everything, but we can so some things and do them very well. With that said, here's my last pep talk for you: Now that you know how to set goals and schedule them into times that fit for you, how to maximize time with social media, and how to be more selective in partnerships, go out there and crush it! Your dreams are waiting for you. And yes, go ahead and take that invite to dinner with a friend. Life is all about balance, so make time for your personal and family life. Your business will thank you!

> It's not a competition to see who can spend the most time on their side hustle. It's all about creating the life *you* want.

4

Lights, Camera, Hustle!

Michelle Ferré

You won't make a lot of money.

That is a phrase I heard from family, friends, and even strangers when I shared my aspirations to be a teacher. That statement haunted me as I spent thousands of dollars pursuing a degree in elementary education. That is a sentiment perpetuated by society that demoralizes teachers as they enter the classroom. That is also a bold-faced lie.

Thankfully I've always been the type of person who loves proving others wrong. I was convinced that my passion for teaching, combined with my strong work ethic, would be enough to open up opportunities for me to make ends meet as a teacher. I knew it was possible, but I needed to find a way to make it a reality.

During my first year of teaching, however, that statement about my lack of income was starting to seem accurate. I had spent hundreds of dollars purchasing books, supplies, decorations, and other seemingly necessary items for my classroom before the school year had even started. I continued to purchase lesson materials on a weekly basis throughout the year in order to provide my students with the educational experiences I knew they deserved. My passion for teaching became a nightmare for my wallet as I fully invested my time and money into my career without any consideration for the impact my actions would have on my financial well-being. I was happy, but I was broke.

Fast forward to the summer leading into my third year of teaching. I had begun to supplement my income by selling digital resources for teachers and was experiencing small levels of success. By selling organizational materials and lesson activities that I had developed to use with my own students, I was suddenly able to fund my iced coffee addiction and purchase new resources for my students without living in fear of the dreaded word "declined" appearing in bold letters as I checked out at the grocery store. The relief I experienced with the small amounts of supplemental income motivated me to continue to seek avenues to monetize my passion and work ethic. I knew compensation would allow me to provide for my students, and I was determined to capitalize on it.

The Start of Vlogging

If you had told me five years ago that I would be running a successful YouTube channel, I would have laughed in your face. As an introvert, the thought of filming myself and putting my life on display for the entire world to see was petrifying. Don't get me wrong, I loved watching other people vlog, or video blog, their lives through a series of videos online. But I had convinced myself that my daily life as a teacher was too repetitive and too mundane to be worth recording. Despite my own self-doubt and despite surrounding myself with reasons not to pursue vlogging, I came to an important realization: Ordinary can be powerful. I didn't have to be the best teacher with the most revolutionary ideas to be able to share my experience online. I just had to be my authentic, ordinary self. I didn't have the most teaching experience, I wasn't the most creative, and I certainly wasn't the funniest (although laughing at my own jokes is my specialty). I was something better: I was relatable.

This realization persuaded me to finally take the leap and begin posting teaching-related videos on my YouTube channel. My initial expectations were low. I merely wanted another outlet to express my overwhelming passion for education, share my genuine teaching experience, and hopefully inspire other teachers in the process. Having experienced the stereotypical "burnout" my first year of teaching, I wanted to show a realistic view of my life as a teacher to better prepare new professionals entering the field. I didn't want to sugarcoat my experience. I wanted other teachers who were feeling disillusioned, unmotivated, and overwhelmed to be able to watch my videos and feel less alone. I was willing to put my shortcomings and mistakes as an educator on display in order to create a community where we as teachers could relate to one another and overcome the difficulties we experienced.

I was fully convinced that vlogging was something I needed to pursue with vigor and passion, so I took the next logical steps. I purchased a camera, designated a spot in my cramped apartment to film, and began creating videos. While I now look back on my first several videos and cringe, I did all the right things. I didn't overthink the technical aspects of filming and instead focused my energy on the most important element: the content. I compiled countless lists of video ideas based on my personal experience as a teacher, and I concentrated my efforts on creating videos that I wish I had access to my first year of teaching. My filming quality definitely could have benefitted from some professional lighting and a backdrop other than my bedroom door, but my early content demonstrated my dedication. I was producing two videos for my channel every week on top of teaching full time, creating educational resources, and fulfilling all of my other adult responsibilities. My spare time, as minimal as it was, became devoted to planning content for future videos so I could continue to expand this newfound passion project. I felt like my purpose in life had expanded, and I was proud of what I was creating.

As a new teacher, I constantly felt inadequate. I needed to personalize learning to fit the needs of every one of my students, I needed to analyze seemingly endless amounts of data to drive my instructional decisions, and I needed to receive additional professional development to stay relevant in the field. I felt like no matter how much effort I put in, I still wasn't competent enough.

Vlogging produced an unfamiliar feeling of pride. I no longer felt inadequate in my work. Rather, I felt empowered by my abilities and used this improved confidence as my motivation. As my channel grew, I became surrounded by individuals who supported and encouraged me. I finally felt understood and accepted for being my authentic self, and that feeling was compelling. My audience appreciated and cared about my ideas, and I was grateful for the opportunity to share them.

Building an Audience

Uploading your first video is a humbling experience. You spend hours filming, editing, and perfecting a video that is only watched by your closest family and friends within the first few hours. The limited number of views and even fewer number of subscribers has you questioning your decision to pursue this new endeavor. You poured your heart and soul into your first video and were convinced this would be enough to immediately acquire thousands of views. However, your confidence did not prepare you for the realities of building an audience.

Rome wasn't built in a day and neither was an audience, especially on YouTube. I've yet to meet a single vlogger who was able to gain thousands of subscribers within their first week posting videos. It just doesn't happen. Building an audience means building trust, and building trust takes time. In order to convince viewers your videos are worth watching, you have to demonstrate your value. Producing viral videos is a great strategy for gaining views but does little to build a relationship with your audience. Establishing a community of loyal and supportive viewers requires purposeful action. As a content creator, it is your responsibility to give your audience a reason to return to your channel.

The most effective tool you have to attract new viewers and gain their trust is your authenticity. In the world of YouTube where anyone with a camera or phone can upload a video, producing original content is imperative. Recreating videos already available online only serves to misguide your audience. Chances are, the original content creator is better suited to produce the videos and will repeatedly outperform you. Don't waste your time pretending to be someone else when you could be building an audience that respects you for who you are. Your potential lies in your original ideas and unique personality. Together, these factors differentiate you from your competitors and help you attract a like-minded audience. Once you have determined your niche, you are able to create videos that serve your audience, provide value, and build trust among your most loyal viewers.

Building a subscriber base is only half the battle. Once you have convinced your audience to follow along with your journey, you have to constantly work to preserve the trust you have established. The value you offer through your content is what first attracted people to watch your video, your personality is what persuaded them to stay, and your consistency is what will maintain your audience over time. A regular upload schedule allows your viewers to anticipate

> The value you offer through your content is what first attracted people to watch your video, your personality is what persuaded them to stay, and your consistency is what will maintain your audience over time.

future videos and trust your ability to generate fresh content. This trust translates into genuine support and initiates monetization opportunities that can propel the success of your personal brand.

Pause and Reflect

Who is your ideal audience? What value do you have to offer them?

Monetizing Your Passion

Think back to the last video you watched online. I would be willing to bet that you spent the first several seconds hovering your mouse over the corner of the video waiting for the "skip ad" button to become available. While the average consumer views commercials as an inconvenience, advertisements are a deserved form of compensation for content creators. The truth is that vlogging can quickly become expensive. Between buying a camera, purchasing editing software, and repairing your camera after you drop it (which will happen, by the way), you can end up shelling out hundreds or even thousands of dollars on equipment. That's not to mention the time you have to spend planning your videos, editing the footage, designing thumbnails, and writing video descriptions. We as teachers all understand how valuable our time is. Without the ability to make money, very few vloggers would continue to create free content for viewers because it simply wouldn't be worth their time and effort. Monetization is compelling. It motivates creators to continue to invest their time in their work, increase their content quality, and produce more videos for their viewers.

Video Advertisements

As a vlogger, monetizing your videos with advertisements is by far the easiest way you can earn supplemental income each month without doing any extra work above and beyond creating videos. Before you are eligible to monetize your videos, you do have to be accepted into the YouTube Partner Program. The requirements to join are constantly changing, but in summary you have to adhere to their policies, live in a region where the program is available, have a minimum number of subscribers, and have a minimum number of watch hours. Once accepted into the program, you will need to link your channel to a Google AdSense account, and then you are ready to start placing advertisements on your videos. If the thought of locating and conducting business with advertisers is enough to make your head spin, don't worry. YouTube makes this process extremely simple. When uploading content, you will have the opportunity to monetize your video with the simple click of a button and will be able to select the advertisement format you would prefer. Your responsibility as a content creator lies in adhering to the community guidelines, understanding copyright, and creating videos that are advertiser-friendly in order to maximize the number of advertisements you can acquire. YouTube takes control of pairing advertisers with your monetized videos and communicates your earnings through your channel analytics. While monetizing your videos with advertisements is the easiest way to earn money as a vlogger, it certainly isn't the most lucrative. Only the top-tier content creators earn enough money from advertisements alone for it to serve as their primary income. Be prepared to seek additional revenue streams in order to generate a profit over and above your expenses as a vlogger.

Partnerships and Sponsorships

Your most valuable asset as a vlogger is your loyal and engaged audience. Having watched hours upon hours of your content, your most faithful viewers feel like they know you personally even though they have never met you. This personal connection with your audience manifests as support, trust, and confidence. A primary opportunity for strengthening or diminishing this trust lies within product recommendations. In recent years, brands have realized the power of influencer marketing and are willing to compensate you for sharing their products and services with your audience. With extensive budgets for marketing, companies can afford to invest immense amounts of money in sponsorships and long-term partnerships with vloggers to promote their products. Plain and simple, this form of monetization can be extremely lucrative. A single sponsorship can bring in the same amount of earnings as several months' worth of advertising revenue. As you begin expanding your opportunities for supplemental income, it is essential that you adopt a business mindset. You have to recognize the value of your influence and ensure that the compensation you receive from brands is worthwhile. While these partnerships can be tricky to navigate, especially in your first few experiences, they are worth exploring. Don't be afraid to reject a sponsorship offer if you feel the company is taking advantage of you or the product will not serve your audience. Any product or service you promote through your videos should provide value to your viewers by making their lives easier or solving a problem they experience. At the end of the day, the trust and loyalty of your audience will always be more valuable than a check you receive in the mail.

Personal Brand Promotion

Building an audience also means building a personal brand. Your morning coffee order, the clothing you wear, your most frequently used phrases, and your personal quirks become associated with your channel. Your viewers come to expect these details in your videos and feel comforted by their presence. These features of your life help form your personal brand. As your channel expands, so does your brand. This growth opens opportunities for you to market products and services you have developed to your audience. The most prevalent example of personal marketing is the promotion of merchandise with your logo, name, or other words and images related to your brand. Supporters of your channel are also eager to purchase any products or services you create that align with your brand and address a pain point. Selling e-books, virtual downloads, and online coaching services are all examples of personal marketing that could be endlessly profitable without the headache of managing and shipping physical goods. This approach to monetization provides you with optimal control over the alignment of the products with your brand and establishes a revenue stream that can be expanded beyond your vlogging platform.

Pause and Reflect

What are some companies or brands that align best with your personal brand and that you could potentially partner with?
What additional products or services could you offer to your audience to make their lives easier?

Making Sacrifices

If I had a dollar for every sacrifice I made while building my brand, I could probably retire from vlogging altogether. While the ability to make money and gain a large following appears glamorous, the work it takes to achieve any level of success certainly is not. From the outside, vlogging appears to be the perfect gig. You carry around a camera, film some short clips of your life, piece them together into a video, and earn money while doing so. But like any other job, the behind the scenes view is strikingly different. Vlogging requires strict commitment, unwavering dedication, and remarkably thick skin to successfully navigate it as a side hustle.

> While the ability to make money and gain a large following appears glamorous, the work it takes to achieve any level of success certainly is not.

It was a Friday night after five long days of teaching, and I was settling into the couch with my favorite takeout dinner to edit my weekly vlog. I spent over six hours uploading video files, sifting through hours of footage, inserting transitions between clips, adding copyright-free music, and exporting the completed video file. I finally vacated the couch at 3:00 in the morning to get a few short hours of sleep before I had to wake up to ensure that my video uploaded correctly since it was scheduled to go live on my channel at 7:00 AM. Repeat this cycle every single Friday for over two years, and you have the exact description of my life as a vlogger. I don't know about you, but the only part of that story that sounded remotely glamorous was the few hours of much-needed sleep.

When I first decided to pursue vlogging, I had a minimal understanding of the substantial time commitment it would be. I didn't realize I would be forfeiting my Friday nights to edit videos to maintain my consistent upload schedule. I didn't know I would have to spend countless hours throughout the week responding to comments and answering emails in order to uphold the connection I had with my audience. I didn't comprehend that vlogging would become the equivalent of another full-time job. I didn't think it would be easy, but I also didn't know it would be this hard.

I've always been an extremely hard worker, but vlogging is mentally and physically exhausting in a unique way. Picking up a camera and recording your daily life becomes monotonous. You can no longer just walk out of your front door and get in your car when you are going to the store. You now have to film yourself grabbing your keys, unlocking and opening your door, stepping onto the porch, closing and relocking your door, walking towards your car, unlocking your car door, getting into the driver's seat, and putting the key into the ignition. You have to repeat this process day in and day out because you're now a vlogger and getting b-roll footage is part of the lifestyle. Your entire routine changes.

You suddenly have to accept private and intimate aspects of your life being made public. By watching your videos, your viewers will learn your name, how many pets you have, what the inside of your house looks like, and more. It can be alarming how much personal information your audience acquires just by observing your life. While you are ultimately in control of what information you make available to the public through your videos, you have to embrace a certain level of vulnerability in order to establish a deep connection with your audience. This exposure can be intimidating and is often met with criticism from viewers as you reveal authentic details of your life.

I vividly remember the first negative comment I received on a video. A viewer wrote that the unevenness of my eyebrows made it difficult for her to continue watching. I stared wide-eyed at the computer screen in disbelief. I spent hours creating a video overflowing with practical tips for teachers, and a stranger was acknowledging a patch of hair on my face. Suddenly my overwhelming passion was not enough to overshadow my insecurities, and that crushed me. In that moment, I began to question whether I had made the right decision to open up my life on the internet. If I was going to continue on this journey as a vlogger, I had to develop a thick skin—and fast.

Documenting your life on video and uploading it for strangers to watch is an invitation for unsolicited scrutiny. The different backgrounds, perspectives, and opinions people hold diversify our world but regularly result in sharp judgments and comparisons. The purchases you make, the emotions you show, and yes, even the shape of your eyebrows are all open targets for criticism on the internet. As human beings, we know it is impossible to please everyone, but that often doesn't stop us from trying.

The reality is that you will make mistakes. You are human and imperfect to a fault. You will say the wrong thing or make a bad decision, and it will be documented for the entire world to see. While these missteps are inevitable, they shouldn't discourage you from capturing your passion on video. Your voice, your ideas, and your identity hold merit and deserve to be shared with the world.

> Your voice, your ideas, and your identity hold merit and deserve to be shared with the world.

Pause and Reflect

How many hours each week are you able to commit to vlogging?
What level of vulnerability are you willing to embrace with your audience?
How will you motivate yourself to continue if you face criticism?

More Than the Money

My mom always warned me not to meet strangers on the internet. Spoiler alert: I didn't listen. Over the years, I've accepted the fact that having thousands of strangers watching my life from all corners of the world is most likely the cause of her increasing number of gray hairs. My mom's hairdresser may disagree, but in my opinion, it is worth it. The ability to collaborate with equally passionate, like-minded individuals has brought me more joy than I ever thought possible. I have been fortunate enough to meet and continually receive inspiration from teachers around the world, which would have been virtually impossible without the connection we formed through my channel. These encounters have widened and positively transformed my perspective as a teacher, content creator, and human being.

My personal evolution has been documented over hundreds of videos spanning a period of several years. If you have looked at an old, awkward picture of yourself and cringed, then you have experienced a fraction of the embarrassment you feel when you watch the first video you ever created. It's painful, trust me. But hidden underneath the discomfort is pride in my personal growth. Vlogging serves as an online diary that captures current thoughts, habits, and emotions. Reflecting on these elements has empowered me to make positive changes in my life that have increased my confidence and enhanced my well-being.

Claiming that vlogging has changed my life is a bold statement that I am willing to make. It is true that I don't know exactly what my life would be like if I had never picked up a camera. But what I do know for certain is that I am happier and more proud of my accomplishments than I ever dreamed I would be. The decision to embark on this lifestyle was made on a whim. I didn't set out on this journey with any specific goals in mind, I didn't consider the sacrifices I would need to make, and I certainly didn't contemplate the ways I could fail. I just followed my passion. That decision turned out to be one of the best choices I have ever made in my life—and it could be the same for you.

5

Write the Book, Already!

Kisha Mitchell

Allow me to introduce myself. I like to say that I am an educator in addition to other things. I hate it when I hear teachers say I am "just a teacher." In my classroom alone, I was an entertainer, motivator, actress, songwriter, counselor, doctor, guide, public speaker, manager, event coordinator, sounding board, IT, CIA, and the FBI. Honestly, what other profession is out here changing lives every day? As educators, we have a myriad of talents that other professions never even dream of! In addition, I am a mother, wife, daughter, daughter-in-law, aunt, cousin, author, podcaster, and educator. I am a person who always knew she had a knack for writing, from the time I used to write silly poems about my big sister, to the time I wrote an 11-page paper in the seventh grade (sorry, Mrs. Johnson, I now understand how much of a pain it was to read all of that!), to the time when people paid me to write their papers in college (you can't blame a girl for trying to get a side hustle early), all the way to the time that I became a sixth- and seventh-grade English Language Arts (ELA) teacher. What you could not tell me, however, was that I would ever become an author. I have always been the type of person to read, but be the person who actually writes books for people to read? *Never!*

Key #1: Don't be afraid to acknowledge that you can actually be a multi-talented human being. It is actually okay to explore more than one talent at a time. Just because you are an amazing teacher doesn't mean that you cannot capitalize on your other hidden gifts!

Thankfully, God places people in your life who can see things in you that you may not be able to see in yourself. The seed of my becoming an author was planted by one of the sweet teachers on my team, Terrie Ponder. She taught social studies, and I taught ELA. We would often do cross-curricular activities and discuss our love for literature. She always impressed me with the variety of cultures that she would introduce to students through diverse literature, such as *Three Cups of Tea*, *Homeless Bird*, and *Red Scarf Girl*. I loved this exposure because I had always noticed how our school-selected novels often lacked a representation of all the unique children I had inside my classroom. I eventually started reading the novels that she had in her classroom for the students we shared.

Around that time, I had my first daughter, and Terrie asked what she could get as a gift. I told her and my other teammate that I would love to have some books with characters that resembled my daughter. So my teammates went searching for a children's book that fit my request. They were shocked by what they realized. With sorrow in their eyes, they told me that they could not find anything. They only found books with animals and with children who did not look like my sweet daughter. Terrie looked at me and said, "You should write a children's book! You are a great writer, and I know you can do this!" Now, I know what you are thinking . . . you think this is when the magic happened. You think this is when I ran home, sat down at my laptop, and banged out my first children's book. You think this seventh-grade ELA teacher, who has always had a love for creative writing, and writing in general, confidently said, "Why, yes, yes I should!" But that was absolutely not my reaction. It was a rushed, "Yeah, right. I have no idea how to do that, and I am just fine teaching kids how to use dazzling description in their narratives without writing something that needs to contain those properties!" I even went on to say these dreaded 12 words: "Maybe one day when I retire, I will give it a shot!" Why do we do that? Why do we always say one day in the far, far future, we will pursue something out of the box and out of our comfort zone, something that takes our breath away at the thought of it? Is it because we think we will be "more mature"? Or is it that our kids will be bigger so then "I will have time"? Or is it due to flat-out fear or self-doubt? I am here to SHOUT TO YOU FROM THE TOP OF MY LUNGS: WRITE THE BOOK, ALREADY, or start the YouTube channel, start the podcast, audition for the part, write the song, whatever that thing is that you have been waiting to do. Don't waste the precious time that you have right this very moment; take the first step towards that thing that has been nudging you!

Pause and Reflect

What is your passion? What topics or activities do you have a strong emotional response to?
How do you bring value to your school, your home, and your community?
What is it that friends are always telling you that you are good at, and you just blow it off as them "just being nice?"
What do you do that makes you feel full of life?

Fear Factor

I have a theory. I believe that the "when I retire" line is a lie we tell ourselves to wiggle out of taking the hard steps to figure out how to do something big and scary. I also believe we say that line because the fear of failure puts a crippling grip on us. The main way to conquer fear is to have courage. But I often found myself choosing comfort over courage. Sometimes we get comfortable where we are. When I got the desire to write a children's book, I was settling in as a graduation coach at a high school, I had my routine down pat, I had a great boss—yes, life was pretty comfortable. I had a successful girls' mentoring group that made me feel fulfilled. I felt as if I were living my purpose by helping the girls in my building. There was always a nudge to impact more girls, but I was afraid to get out of my comfort zone. When the whispering of writing the book came, I told God, out loud, "yeah, yeah, maybe one day when I get finished doing all the things I am working on." The thought of trying to learn to do something new made me feel both uncomfortable and afraid. But the downfall to comfort is complacency. Complacency was making me unable to recognize the talents that I had and the things that I was doing uniquely.

> But the downfall to comfort is complacency. Complacency was making me unable to recognize the talents that I had and the things that I was doing uniquely.

Key #2: Complacency can make you unable to recognize unique gifts that you take for granted.

But one day, my courage finally did kick in. I realized I had identified a cause/topic that made me passionate, inspired, and ticked off. I believed that if I *didn't* write about it, I would be letting not only myself down, but also my two daughters. The turning point was when my daughter was the sweet, tender age of three years old. A little girl in her class told her that her brown skin was not beautiful. Yep, just like that. "Your brown skin isn't beautiful." It was so direct, so specific, so simple, yet so devastating to my little brown girl. After my sweet girl retold me this story while sitting at the dinner table, my mind was racing. I felt anger, sadness, disappointment, and hurt. Since my daughter had entered the world, I did everything I could to speak positivity to her. Raising a self-confident daughter—when all of the messages and images in the world are telling her that she should be something else—is already hard enough. Because I use writing to help me process things and vent, I went to my room and I started writing. I mean I wrote and wrote and wrote. What I was writing was several love letters to my little girl to tell her how beautiful she was and how much she had to offer the world. Of course, I shared this devastating news with my village. We searched high and low to find a book that would counter this negative seed that had been planted in my daughter's mind, but we could find only one book at that time. At that moment, I thought of Toni Morrison's words, "If there is a book that you want to read, but it hasn't been written yet, you must be the one to write it." This quote rang in my ears and my heart. I felt the sudden nudge that perhaps all those things I wrote to my sweet girl in my journal needed to be turned into a children's book. The only problem was that I did not see myself as *writer* . . . I teach children how to write. I am no author!

Fear. Fear. Fear. Fear.

But wait. Maybe I can be. It all came to me so simply. My youngest daughter, who was only a few months old at the time, loved, loved, loved reading *Brown Bear, Brown Bear, What Do You See?* Every. Single. Night. I was listening to the words and it hit me! *Brown Girl, Brown Girl, What Do You See?* If Bill Martin could write about a brown bear, surely, *surely*, I could write about a brown girl, right? But wait, people will think I am racist if I pointedly say "brown girl." I finally had to decide that I belonged to myself (thank you Brené Brown!) and not to anyone else—not to my parents, husband, or career. I had to have the courage to speak my family's truth, my truth, and my daughter's story, and never change who I truly am along the way. I had to finally realize that my story was valuable and worth telling! I had to convince myself that producing a counter-argument to the negative statement made to my child would be a privilege for others to hear and could ultimately help someone.

Fear. Fear. Fear. Fear. Fear. Fear. Fear. Fear. Fear.

But after all that inspiration, I yet again talked myself out of writing the book that had come to my heart.

It just so happens that around this same time, one of my abso-lute favorite cousins was diagnosed with metastatic breast cancer. And, with this diagnosis, God birthed a vision in her to create a Christian-based t-shirt company. She listened to the nudging and, boy, did her company boom! It was called Fight Apparel. And the debut shirt was a shirt with these words on it: Faith Over Fear. Wow, did she nail it for this season in my life. I was being crippled by fear, so I immediately ordered one. We met at Chick-fil-A for the delivery and I shared with her what God had laid on my heart to do. She looked me in the eyes and told me very pointedly, "Don't wait until you have been diagnosed with stage IV breast cancer before you finally do what God has told you to do." Immediately, I burst into tears right there at our high-top table next to the window. I knew at that moment that I could not ignore what God had shown me to do.

Key #3: Decide that right now is the right time . . . not later. Don't wait. Whatever God has placed on your heart, don't live in fear and put it off!

Courage to Leap!

"Everyone has a story to tell, the question is will you have the courage to tell yours?" This quote by Maya Angelou hit me square in the face in the midst of my decision-making process of whether or not I could actually be an author. I had a story, something that inspired me, but I truly, truly had so much fear of putting it in writing. Because I am an educator, there are so many unspoken rules that are applied to us. My story was one that speaks to a little girl's heart, that any girl who had been teased or taunted because of a physical attribute could relate to. My topic just so happens to deal with a topic that many people are afraid to discuss: skin color. As I was going through this internal struggle and debate over whether to pull the trigger on my children's book, I was reading the book *You Are a Badass* by Jen

Sincero. I came to the page that said in very large print "DO NOT WASTE YOUR PRECIOUS TIME GIVING A SINGLE CRAP ABOUT WHAT ANYBODY ELSE THINKS OF YOU." To that, I responded a loud, "YEAH!" in my head. In all honesty, I had to tell myself that my book was not written with the intent to harm anyone; it was written to empower and encourage girls to see what is beautiful and unique about themselves and to teach others how to appreciate the differences of those around them. These reasons resonate so greatly with what schools and teachers try so hard to instill in their students: kindness and acceptance.

Key #4: Decide on your content, on what makes you tick, on what gets you excited, angry, or sad. What is your inspiration? Brainstorm and get pen to paper!

Once you have written your story, it is human nature to want to share your excitement, your story, and your vision with others. Of course, whenever we are working on something new—a new concept, a new tool, or a new strategy—we love to get validation from others. And as teachers, most of us are natural collaborators. I caution you, though, on collaborating, sharing, and getting feedback on your thoughts and ideas on your potential product. You could find yourself in a situation where anyone who has given even the slightest input may come back and try to lay claim to your creation or your idea. Unfortunately, I had to learn this the hard way. Because I am not a natural at business ventures, I did not cover my bases by getting any dealings I had with outside entities written down in a contract. I, unfortunately, utilized a friend to help me with marketing because, as a self-publisher, you must market yourself. Somewhere along the way, there was a misunderstanding. Because we had not had our expectations and arrangements in writing, it ended up ending our friendship.

At that point, my topic had already shown itself, and I had already written my story (remember the journaling). With my writing complete, I had to make a few decisions on next steps. I had no idea how to do them! But as educators, we have unique research skills that others may not have. So, I said a prayer that was something like this: *Okay, Lord, you are going to have to show me how to do this and put the resources in place so that I can do what you told me to do.*

Step by Step by Step

I began researching. The first question I had is important for aspiring authors to ask: Does anyone have a book with the title I have in mind? Trusty Google said no, but there was one more place I could look to verify the information: Copyright.org. This fun little site is not only where you can find out whether or not someone has your title but also where you can make sure that you keep legal rights to your own words! So once I edited my manuscript a few times, I uploaded it and paid my fee to have my work copyrighted. You will also need to purchase a UPC code if you ever have the goal of selling your book. There are some sites that have deals where you can purchase copyright and UPC together. You know we all love combo deals.

The next order of business was to determine whether I wanted to self-publish independently, through Amazon or other self-publishing/on-demand publishing sites, or get published the traditional way through a publishing house. There were pros and cons to them all, and I will take a second to outline what I found. Of course, the choice is completely yours!

There are some major questions to ask yourself: Is this goal just something you want to check off the bucket list, is it something you want to turn around quickly, or is it something you want to turn into a side hustle? For me, I absolutely wanted my book to be more than just a book. I wanted it to be a movement that reached little girls in communities across America and make money while doing it. I wanted my book to be something with a personal touch where I could meet people face to face and spread love to parents, teachers, and students who struggle with self-esteem issues—wait, that sounds like what we do as teachers! You are exactly right! And truth be told, I would absolutely go into schools and give this book away if it weren't for my very business-minded husband. As good humans, we often feel guilty making money off of our talents. Our hearts just want to help people and have an impact. But why do we think that it is a sin to make money while doing so?

Key #5: Give yourself permission to make money from your intellectual property, that is, anything that comes from your brain and that helps people become better humans! Wow, that is GENIUS!

Back to the publishing question: I decided to self-publish. With that route, it relieves the pressure of trying to "sell" your idea to a traditional publishing house. You also get all of your own profits. You do, however, have more of an upfront financial investment in the printing of your own books. This could range from $5 or less for a small paperback book up to $15 per book for a hardcover book. Just like with other large purchases, the larger volume you purchase, the less your cost is. There are several printers from which to choose . . . you could go local, or you could order from China. It truly just depends on how long you want to wait. And if you are ordering from China, the bulk of your cost is going to be for shipping, not cost per book. The challenge of printing in bulk is storage, but Amazon is so amazing that they offer a Fulfillment by Amazon option for small businesses or self-publishers. So, that is always an option if you're afraid of purchasing in bulk.

In addition, if you self-publish, you need to hire an illustrator, as opposed to working with a publishing house which would pair you with an illustrator. If you are in need of an illustrator, you could join Facebook groups, look up children's book illustrators on Instagram, or go on Fiverr or the like. On all of those avenues, getting an illustrator is as simple as sending an inbox message. Fees will vary based on your illustrator's experience and skillset and the type of illustrations you may want. Some important questions to ask your illustrator:

1. Do you provide character sketches?
2. Do you like heavy author input, or would you rather just go for it on your own?
3. How many characters are included in your price?
4. Do you provide a timeline?
5. Do you charge by the page, or is your price based on pages in the entire book?
6. Are you also a graphic artist? (This is valuable because if the answer is yes, then this person can also design your cover, words, and word placement on your pages within your children's book, if they have this skill; if not, you will need to hire a graphic artist.)
7. What are your payment options?

Once you have chosen your illustrator and have received all of your artwork, you must make sure that your illustrator sends you your files in the dimensions and format that your chosen self-publishing company requires. Here are some options for on-demand companies to research: AuthorHouse, CreateSpace, Lulu, and Xlibris (and, of course, Amazon provides these services, as well). With on-demand companies, you do not have to house your inventory. But there is no guarantee that your product will be high-quality, so definitely ask for samples from any publishing company you use. Another advantage to using this route is that it is low-cost and low-risk. If the cost of printing is an obstacle you need to overcome, you can always go to Kickstarter, DonorsChoose, or GoFundMe to generate funds. Your publisher will send you a draft of what your final product will be to ensure quality printing, ink, and color. And then, if you are paying for bulk printing, you wait on your order to be completed. If you're working with an on-demand publisher, then that is the final step! You can begin selling! When I finally got those samples in my hands, it was in that moment I realized that I was actually an author!

Key #6: Ask yourself: Is this goal something you just want to check off the list, is it something you want to turn around quickly, or is it something you want to turn into a side hustle?

Vulnerability Releases Creativity: Starting a Podcast

The truth of the matter is that the skills that we take for granted (or assume that anyone in this world can do) are actually valuable skills that people will pay money to read and/or hear. It is okay to monetize your story. Your story may come through

> The truth of the matter is that the skills that we take for granted (or assume that anyone in this world can do) are actually valuable skills that people will pay money to read and/or hear.

a children's book, novel, blog, or podcast. The challenge is to choose the right medium and get your story out there! I had to allow myself to be vulnerable. Doing so allowed for even more creativity to rise from within me: more books, a podcast, and now a curriculum. Have the courage to tell your story. I saw that my children's book was having an impact on people and that my story was something that people needed. It made me realize that as an educator, mom, wife, friend, and entrepreneur, I had additional life experiences that could help others. The idea for my podcast Sweet Tea and Sunshine was born from that realization.

Podcasting is yet another way you can monetize your story. Most of us as human beings are experiencing the same types of things. But what normally happens is that we operate in silos, never sharing our stories because we feel like we are the only people going through those things. Telling your story through the medium of your choice could potentially help someone who is suffering in silence because they have no one to talk to. That is what I learned through my wide range of experiences and the feedback I received.

When we began our podcast, it was formed under the premise that there are some wives who don't have a support group of married women, and they feel like they are failing at marriage because they assume they are the only ones experiencing certain things. Then we thought about educators who may not have anyone to trust in their schools to discuss things with. So we thought that we would discuss issues that teachers encounter, but instead of staying in a negative space about it, we'd acknowledge those challenges while also offering up some solutions. My friend, who is a teacher, and I thought that it would be genius for us to have discussions that offered up an administrator's point of view and a teacher's. So, we started this journey on one outlet called Spreaker. Then we moved to SoundCloud, and finally we filled out a proposal to Apple iTunes, and we were accepted! If you are going to start a podcast, you need to identify the target audience and your topic. One challenge that we faced was that we wanted to be everything to everybody. We needed to focus our ideas and home in on our audience and topics. Many people don't know this, but you can monetize your podcast once you reach 10,000 downloads or have 500 subscribers, and then you can begin getting advertisers! YouTube is a necessary accessory to your podcast in order to get your subscribers where you want them.

Being a self-published author and podcaster, or starting your own business in general, takes a certain level of grit and hustle. As a self-published author, I had to look for events to set up and be a vendor, and because I had an additional vision to go along with my books, I had to seek out creative avenues in which to place my book. Through this creative process, I landed an opportunity to work with Atlanta's WNBA team, the Atlanta Dream. They allowed me to sell my books at their home games periodically for *free*, something that normally cost $500. The reason they did this was that they believed in the message that I was sending through my children's books. This led to me meeting several parents and children at my vending table who also had daughters who experienced something similar to what my daughter did. They felt that their daughters were dealing with a negative self-image and that my book addressed some of those issues. At every event I did, whether I read at a local library or went to conferences and met teachers who were interested in my book, it was reaffirmed over and over that this story was valuable and worth sharing. Through the relationships I built with the Atlanta Dream, I was allowed the opportunity to be the main contributor for their diversity and inclusion pillar of their core beliefs. I, along with members of the Dream, traveled through metro Atlanta and used my children's books to teach children from a variety of backgrounds to love themselves first and love and appreciate the differences of others. If I had not told our story, then I would not have been able to touch lives beyond my building. We are life changers.

Key #7: Give yourself permission to pivot.

Balancing Act

I am so very thankful that I honored myself as a multi-talented person and acknowledged my skills. I impacted not only my students but others and made money doing it! This did not come without some sacrifices. I lost a business partner and friend; I had to stay up late nights recording podcasts and of course deal with mommy and wifey guilt. Is wifey guilt really a thing? But the way that I overcame the mommy guilt was by involving my daughters in the entire process. It has allowed us to have intellectual conversations about everything from having your own business, to tapping into your creativity and producing something amazing, to learning how to sell! My now nine-year-old has been telling her *own* story behind the vending table when people stop by. She is articulate, confident, and excited to tell her story. She has been doing it since she was five years old, and I can only hope that these are seeds that will blossom into a mighty oak tree of confidence in her life! Perhaps because of her involvement in this adventure, she will not have to overcome the fear that I once faced—and still face in owning my story! I know that she sees me because I was a little sad leaving to even co-write this fabulous book, and I had a talk with her. I said, "I feel bad leaving you and your sister this weekend." She said, "Don't feel bad mommy! Every time you leave, I know you are working on something amazing!" That statement was so important to me. She checked on me every night that I was writing my chapter, and she checked in with me the following morning to see how far I had gotten. I had to understand that my children seeing me work hard and own my self is also good parenting!

> I had to understand that my children seeing me work hard and own my self is also good parenting!

Key #8: Owning yourself and recognizing what is uniquely special about yourself is also good parenting.

6

From Teacher to Content Creator

Kristen Donegan

Growing up in the 1980s, I knew I always wanted to be a teacher. I was that kid digging through my teacher's trash can for dried up Expo markers, extra book orders, and copies so I could play school at home with the whiteboard I had begged my grandparents to get me for Christmas. If the neighborhood kids were busy, I'd use my sister or Barbies as students. I could play school for hours.

When I wasn't playing school, I was also finding ways to make money. Inspired by *The Baby-Sitters Club*, I put up fliers in our neighborhood, sold hot dogs and lemonade on the corner, and built roller coasters and haunted houses and charged kids an entrance fee. I did chores around our house and cleaned houses with my mom. I don't even remember what I was saving up for as a kid, but according to my momma, I liked selling things. Being an entrepreneur was natural to me. I really liked it, and I was pretty darn good at it!

Fast forward to 2008, my fourth year of teaching. I was teaching first grade, was in the middle of my master's program with an emphasis in reading, and was finally tenured! I was in my groove of teaching . . . finally. By this time, I had figured out my teaching style, had strong classroom management, and was feeling confident in my ability as a teacher. I took some of my knowledge from my master's program and created family literacy nights for the families and teachers at our school.

I was also teaching paid professional development classes for our district and helping teachers create engaging lessons. I showed them how to set up literacy centers efficiently to meet the needs of all learners, use technology in a meaningful way, and turn our district word study lessons to a digital format so that students learning English could increase their vocabulary. I even started selling the digital lessons to teachers who didn't want to make them from scratch.

I was happy. I was living out my childhood dream . . . until the pink slips (a layoff notice) went out . . . again. You see, every spring, newer teachers received the dreaded pink slip, which let us know that our position wouldn't be available the next school year. I freaked out the first year I got one. But eventually, I didn't take them seriously because by the end of the school year, our positions were always there, and our pink slips were always rescinded. Until they weren't.

At the end of the 2008 school year, more than 400 tenured teachers in my district were laid off. Since many of us were hired on the same date, our district had us draw straws, literally, to determine our call-back number in case a position opened up. We began collecting unemployment and were put on our district's substitute teacher list. Nothing felt more degrading at the time than working on a master's degree and subbing for teachers you were training the year before, for a measly $90 per day. I was crushed.

I knew that teaching didn't bring in a large paycheck, but this new unemployment thing meant I was broke! It was worse than being *teacher poor*. I did what I could to make ends meet. I got myself a roommate, started pet-sitting, tutored students, sold my car, became a nanny thanks to Craigslist, and even rented out my home as a vacation rental.

Then I began looking at what I had created during my professional development sessions and my master's program and knew I wanted to monetize these things—or make money from them.

Can I Make Extra Money From This?

Could I actually earn any money from the things I was already creating? Well, I was ready to find out! I created a very basic website using GoDaddy and linked it to my PayPal account. At that moment, Easy Teaching Tools was born. I remember being so excited to design it and make it my own. I downloaded every free design element and font I could get my hands on to add to my site. At the time, I thought it looked very professional. But looking back at my first site, I cringe. It wasn't pretty. In fact, it was a mess! But it didn't matter; it was mine. It couldn't be taken away from me because of budget cuts and district layoffs.

I started selling my supplemental materials to support emerging bilingual students, I turned my master's thesis into a *Family Literacy Handbook* for teachers, and I sold the digital word study lessons.

It was all very do-it-yourself and wasn't very pretty! I had no clue how to create PDFs so I would print out the materials and then scan them, one-by-one, to make one PDF document. When someone would place an order, I'd burn the materials onto a CD, create a CD label, stamp my logo onto it, and pop it in the mail. I was so proud of myself and this little hobby I had going.

At the time, I knew nothing about marketing, and people weren't using social media to drive traffic like they do now. It just wasn't a thing in 2009. I just crossed my fingers and *hoped* teachers would magically come across my website. Some did, but it was few and far between.

I wish I could say that selling on my own website helped alleviate the financial burden I faced as an unemployed teacher, but it didn't . . . yet.

After subbing for a year, I was hired to teach in Hawai'i. I packed up my life within two short weeks. It was another dream of mine, so I went for it! I packed up two pieces of luggage and two boxes of essential teaching stuff and moved my life over to O'ahu. I didn't have housing lined up, so I stayed in a hotel for a week. I arrived on a Friday and started teaching the following Monday. It was crazy but so exciting! Eventually, I found a home and was able to move my dog over during winter break. I made sure to leave school each day and go do something outdoors, whether it was hiking, surfing, or running and breathing in that salty island air.

I loved my time teaching there but, my goodness, it was expensive. The cost of living was outrageous, and my teaching salary was 20% less than what I was earning in Southern California. Since we were in the middle of the ocean, it was expensive to buy the things we take for granted at our local teaching supply stores, grocery stores, and Target. I ate a lot of cereal for dinner that year, as it was all I could afford. Plus, I had only one sale from my website that entire year. I tried to tutor on the island, but it was impossible to find clients. I was broke and lonely, so I eventually moved back home.

Once back in Orange County, California, I was hired to teach a half combo . . . the day before school started . . . an hour away . . . the year Common Core was being implemented. I was scrambling trying to find resources for my classroom since I had sold most of my teaching stuff when I left Hawai'i.

Finding a Better Way

During this time, one of my close friends asked whether I had heard about a website called Teachers Pay Teachers (TpT). I hadn't but was intrigued. I checked it out and couldn't believe that it had what I was already doing, but was so much better! And there was even an option to create digital downloads rather than hard copies, like I had been doing on my website. That meant no more burning CDs and mailing them out. And to think I wasn't sure whether going digital would be best. So glad I went that route!

Over the next couple of months, I became a bit obsessed with creating things I needed for my classroom. I downloaded all of the free fonts, clipart, borders, and backgrounds to use in my teaching resources. I felt the same way I did when I discovered that Microsoft Word had clipart and thematic borders. I went a little crazy!

My school lacked core curriculum and supplemental materials, so I created them for my students. I made differentiated math and language arts centers and different art projects that matched our unit themes, and I came up with resources to help me organize a combo class. I loved creating, but it came at a cost:

- ◆ I often missed out on weekend fun with my friends, either because I was too tired from staying up late during the week creating or because I wanted to stay at home to create.
- ◆ I lacked major balance in my life.
- ◆ I spent most of my free time creating resources, which meant I wasn't working out or cooking healthy meals.
- ◆ It was hard for me to be present because I was constantly thinking about my to-do list.
- ◆ There was always so much to do that it was impossible to do everything well, which was a hard concept for me.

I was creating a lot, blogging on my website, and slowly implementing social media strategies. I slowly began growing a following of teachers who liked what I was putting out. But *success didn't come overnight.* At first, I was making enough money to pay my cell phone bill every month and buy extra teaching supplies and resources for my classroom. I looked at this new hobby income as "fun money" to do the things I couldn't always afford with my teaching salary alone. Eventually, I was able to pay for my car payment and ultimately my rent and summer trips thanks to *this hobby that was slowly turning into a side hustle.* It took at least four years and a lot of hard work.

Pause and Reflect

What are you willing to give up in order to create teaching content for others?

Homing In on What I Was Good At

While creating, I was all over the map. I was making lots of things but hadn't really found *my thing*—you know, the *thing* I was really good at and the *thing* teachers really needed. Plus, I needed a *thing* that everyone wasn't already creating and sharing. Everyone was creating centers, classroom decor, games, and assessments on TpT. I wanted to create something different.

But then I started creating things that saved teachers time. They were simple things like editable classroom lists, assignment slides for transitions, and a year-long memory book that students were in charge of rather than the teacher. I was writing blog posts about different organization hacks I came up with that made my life easier.

I thought what I was creating was too simple, and I remember thinking, "Teachers are already doing this, I don't need to be sharing this with them." But here's what I learned. Don't assume! The thing that you think others already know or already do in their classrooms, they most likely don't! They need your ideas!

> The thing that you think others already know or already do in their classrooms, they most likely don't! They need your ideas!

I started sharing these ideas on Instagram at my account, @easyteachingtools, in my newsletter to teachers, and in various blog posts. Teachers would often comment how my ideas were helping them in their classroom, and I just couldn't believe it. Some of these posts went viral—which means that the idea spread quickly and had a positive reaction from teachers. The more that happened, the more I realized that I was onto something. Teachers needed what I was sharing!

So I turned some of the ideas into a professional development session and began presenting my tips around the United States. The doubts I had about whether teachers were already doing what I was sharing went away after I received feedback. Teachers in my sessions weren't doing these things in their classroom . . . yet. Teachers were blown away, and I kept hearing over and over again how these ideas were "game changers" in their classrooms. The impact I was having on these teachers and their students across the country was *big*. And at that moment, everything made sense. You see, I had a principal who believed in me. When I was laid off, he wrote my letter of recommendation and said, "Kristen is a leader in and out of the classroom. She is destined to serve in educational roles of increasing scope and influence." At the time, I didn't know what he meant. But after seeing how I was helping, and I mean *truly helping*, teachers, I understood exactly what he meant.

Pause and Reflect

Is there an area of teaching that you're really good at? It can be content-related or related to classroom set-up, student relationships, classroom management, etc.

From Teacher to Course Creator

I wanted to reach more teachers, so I took my ideas and created a paid, online course. Easier said than done, I know! I actually listened to a lot of entrepreneur podcasts and purchased a business course that showed me how to do this. Then I started putting it all together.

Here's what the process looked like:

◆ I polled teachers on Instagram and in my Facebook group to see what they were struggling with in their classroom. I wanted to really help solve their problems. I asked them what their biggest struggles were. I wanted to know what teaching was like for them with these struggles, and I wanted to know what teaching would be like if they were to find a solution for these problems.

◆ I took their answers, word for word, and created a course outline that I thought would help solve their problems. This outline was what I used to create the course content. I took their problems and used those as the course modules. Then I came up with solutions, and those were my lessons inside each module.

◆ I combined the course outline with one of my professional development PowerPoint slideshows. That meant I opened up the PowerPoint presentation and added more slides from the course outline so that it flowed together.

◆ I used screencast software to record my PowerPoint presentation, or slideshow. I had no idea it could be so easy. I opened up PowerPoint, plugged in an external microphone, and recorded myself talking. It was great because I could do it in my pajamas from the comfort of my bed—makeup and brushed hair weren't required!

◆ I used my ring light and soft box lighting and turned my office into a "studio." This meant I could record anytime of the day, and the lighting helped me look fresh and professional.

◆ I used my basic iPhone to record myself talking. No fancy camera equipment was necessary. I attached my iPhone to the ring light and began talking away! When I was finished with each lesson, I airdropped it from my iPhone to my MacBook. If that's not an option for you, you can email the video to yourself.

◆ I sent the screencast and the recordings of me talking to a video editor overseas, which was less expensive than hiring someone in the United States. You can find freelancers overseas for $4 to $25 an hour. If you were to hire in the United States, it would be at least $100 an hour. If hiring for this task isn't in your budget, you can edit the videos yourself using video editing software.

♦ I hired an assistant to take the finished videos and add them onto my course platform as lessons. I also had my assistant do other tasks for me that saved me a lot of time so I could focus on creating content.

♦ I used many of the resources from TpT along with brand new resources and added them into my course.

♦ I created a sales page and used some of the exact wording from the teachers I polled in the very beginning. Using their wording helped touch on the pain points that teachers were experiencing and made them think, "It's like she's inside of my head. I need her help!"

♦ I started promoting the course to teachers in my Facebook groups, on my Instagram page, and in my newsletter. I created Facebook ads so I could reach more teachers.

During that very first launch, I had a goal of being able to help 20 teachers. I ended up helping over 100 that very first time. And when I opened enrollment for a second time, I had 150 more sign up. Not only was I transforming their lives, but I was making enough money to pay for all our bills, while being able to stay at home with a new baby.

The most rewarding part of all of this was our exclusive Facebook group for course members. Teachers were able to ask questions, get feedback, share their progress, and collaborate. During each session, I'd do *live* trainings inside the course based on what they needed extra support with. I loved how much we were able to interact. I typically don't know who's reading my blogs posts and only get an hour with teachers when I'm presenting professional development. But with this online course, we really got to know one another on a deeper level and connect!

I also found their feedback, submitted through our Facebook group and a survey after the course, to be remarkable. Teachers shared that this course was transformative, it helped them fall in love with teaching again, and it helped them get organized so they could focus on teaching. They were able to leave school at a reasonable time and still have time to do the things they love outside of the classroom, like work out, go to their child's soccer game, and cook a real meal. Remember earlier when I thought my ideas were too simple or people were already using them? Well, the feedback and the results these teachers were getting only affirmed what I finally believed, *I can truly help teachers.*

Pause and Reflect

Now that you have a list of areas that you're pretty good at, let's home in. Circle one or two of the teaching areas that you really want to share with other teachers.

Next Steps

If I can do it, so can you! I've shared a bit about my journey to get where I am now. Here are some action steps you can take to get on your way to transforming the lives of teachers who really need you.

Create a Business Name

I often get asked how I came up with my business name, Easy Teaching Tools. I really wish I knew the answer. To be honest, I don't remember how it came about. But the crazy thing is that I look at where I was when I created it 10 years ago and the resources and course I'm creating today, and it totally fits. When you create your name, consider leaving out your grade level, because that will limit what you can do with your audience. Also, check to make sure that name isn't already being used online.

Set Up Social Media Accounts

Once you decide on a name, check to make sure that name isn't taken on Facebook, Instagram, Twitter, and Pinterest. If it's available, create accounts on social media. It doesn't mean you have to use it right away, but it will be there when you're ready. Plus, it eliminates the chance of someone else using that name. When you are ready, start using your accounts to post images, articles, and stories that will resonate with your audience. Post consistently to help grow and connect with your audience.

Find Your "Thing"

The more you create, interact with other teachers, and get feedback, the clearer your "thing" will become. I wish I could tell you exactly what to focus on, but it's not that easy. This

> The more you create, interact with other teachers, and get feedback, the clearer your "thing" will become.

part is about you, what you're good at, and the teachers you serve. What are you passionate about? What's something you're always complimented on?

Test It Out

As you're sharing what you know, check to see whether it's working. It's a lot like teaching—we reflect on the lesson, check our students' progress, and get feedback. You can also do that with your audience of teachers. It can be as simple as asking them, "What do you think?" It also works well to create a Google Form and collect feedback that way. You can take that information and move forward. Your audience will tell you what they need, so really consider listening to them!

Create Your Course

Once you've tested out your resources, blog posts, and content, use the information from polling your audience and start creating. Decide how you want to get your content out to the teachers who want it. There are many platforms like Kajabi, Teachable, and Kartra to host your course. Do your research and find the platform that fits your budget and needs. There is so much information online to help you set it all up.

I'm so excited for you to share your knowledge with other teachers. They need you, trust me! If you're feeling excited but a bit scared as you embark on this journey, ignore that voice in your head . . . it's just a story! You are meant for great things! You've already impacted the lives of your students who've been fortunate to have you as their teacher. Imagine being able to impact even more students by inspiring, supporting, and collaborating with their teachers. I believe in you!

> Imagine being able to impact even more students by inspiring, supporting, and collaborating with their teachers.

7

The Millionaire Teacher's Mindset

Kayse Morris

A Day in the Life of a Teacher

It's 5:00 AM, and the alarm from my iPhone begins to buzz. I hit the neon orange snooze button a few more times than I should. Ready or not, I roll out of bed with my frizzy, wired top knot of blonde hair. I search like a circus mime for my glasses on my nightstand. Luckily, after a few minutes, I find them and stumble into the kitchen to start my Keurig, in hope that it can revive my lifeless body. It's another Monday, but I'm determined to make it matter. After my first sip of coffee, I jump in the shower. My boys have to be at school at 7:00 AM so I can make the trek across our little town to my school. It's the price I have to pay for being able to drop them off myself, instead of waking up earlier to put them on one of the 80 school buses in my hometown.

Fast forward to 7:43 AM. My wheels make charcoal black marks in the parking lot as they squeal across the pavement. I'm two minutes early and am rushing to punch the proverbial clock that's not even a clock these days, but a computer software system that tracks my every move. I'm not worried about my day because my lesson plans were finalized last week during another painful yet productive faculty meeting.

I'm not like other teachers at my school, and I haven't figured out why yet. I follow the beat of my own drum. I work strictly for the kids instead of the system. In true "Harry Wong" fashion, I greet my students every morning, so I'm standing in the rectangular frame of my classroom door ready to tackle the day. I can smell the exhaust from the buses as the adult-sized kids begin to pile into the hallway. The middle school teacher at the door barks orders at each of them, as she does on a daily basis: "Stop talking! Walk on the red line! Take off your hood! Go get breakfast!" It's a typical chant that I hear from fellow teachers and, if I'm being honest, it makes my skin crawl.

My main mission is to turn this entire process upside down. I've never been to a school with positive vibrations or met a teacher like Miss Honey from *Matilda*, but if I know anything about life it's that I can shake up this twisted game and make sure my students know how much I love them.

"Use your words for good, Kayse." That's what I tell myself each morning before my first student walks in the door. Then I see her. One of the hundreds of students who changed my life. It's Maria, with the pitch-black perfect hair. She enters the building clothed from head to toe in fashion, and I know the deeper story about how her parents work hard to provide her with those things.

"Hey Maria! Good morning! How'd that soccer game go yesterday? I'm digging those earrings. If you're hungry, grab some breakfast and we can work on that essay you're going to make an A on."

Maria isn't like most students either. Her smile is electric, and the dimples on the side of her cheeks tell a story like I've never heard. Her parents immigrated to the United States before she was born, and they constantly push 100-hour work weeks to provide for her and her brothers and sisters. One day we had a parent meeting with her dad to show him Maria's potential if she focused on her studies. I'll never forget that day. I cried more during that meeting than I've ever cried at any meeting. Her dad entered in my classroom with dirty knee pads and paint all over his clothes. He came straight from laying carpet and painting houses to check in on his daughter. In his broken English, he painted the story of how he immigrated to the United States to make a better life for his daughter. A tear fell down his cheek as he began to outline each and every hour he worked to make her life meaningful. My mindset changed in that instant. I had always wanted the best for Maria, but before that meeting, I didn't see the bigger picture. I just wanted her to study more. Now I wanted her to have everything her heart desired.

Luckily, I had the privilege of teaching Maria for two years as a sixth grader and as an eighth grader, and I followed her journey as her parents became American citizens. Maria's is just one of the stories that changed my life. Her passion for life, coupled with her parents' deep desire to want more for her, made me realize that I, too, had a passion: helping children and teachers as much as possible.

Fast forward to a few years into my teaching journey. I was beginning to lose my bursting pride that made me Miss Honey–like. The gratification I used to have from teaching was fizzling and fading fast, and I couldn't figure out why. I was struggling through what I now know was postpartum depression after having two blue-eyed baby boys 12 months and 11 days apart. My days used to be filled with blue skies, green grass, and trans-formational teaching, but now they began to fade into black and white. No more blue skies, no more bubbling personality. I just felt lost in a sea of dark, depressed water, and my job pulled me deeper into the unknown.

Instead of swimming through the waves and feeling the sun on my skin, I became angry. My anger started with the teacher next door who sat down all day and still earned the same pay-check I did. Next, I became frustrated with the system. I let other teachers grab me like tiny crabs in a bucket, using their claws to pinch me back down before I could escape. Don't you see? I let those people get to me. Each day become a cycle that went like this: Wake up, hang out in my crab bucket, repeat. I was struggling to write lesson plans each day, and I realized I had become my worst nightmare.

I was complacent.

What I didn't know was that the trajectory of my life would change forever. Complacency took me through the world wide web each day finding lesson plans that were already created, so I could swipe my imaginary teacher debit card and have someone else do the work for me. It was easy. I was complacent. A quick search on the internet took me to a website where I could pay a few hundred pennies and have my day mapped out for me.

Hell yes!

I began buying lesson plans online in the hope of making my life easy, normal, and less depressed. Little did I know that I would actually find myself again. Each day got a little better because I began using these lesson plans to find my fire in the classroom, a fire that had been put out by raging waters of depression. Although I didn't realize it at the time, it was as if the grey sky began to fade into color again.

Then it happened: the day that changed my life forever. If I'm being honest, I suppose it was a series of moments, but this moment deserves an entire chapter in my book of life when I finally reach those pearly gates of Heaven. This moment will be my Olympic medal, my World Series trophy, my *me* moment of all time.

The Paradigm Shift

It was a random fall Georgia evening in October 2013. I was watching trashy reality television and drinking a beer with my husband when I decided to start making my own resources to sell online.

I looked over at my husband and jokingly, albeit slightly tipsy, said, "I like using these new lesson plans in the classroom and I think it's something I could actually do myself."

In a true husband fashion, he said, "Go for it. I think it'll be good for you."

That sweet southern drawl coming from my tall, bearded principal of a husband turned my dark, depressed demeanor into a millionaire teacher mindset.

I got off to a slow start conquering my abundant ocean of funk, but at least it was a start. Unbeknownst to me, I began taking pieces of depression one by one, crumbling them in my mind, and throwing them in my theoretical trash can. I'd grab a new piece every day. I'd slowly scroll through it in my mind, ball it up, and throw it away. Change didn't happen overnight, but each day I felt lighter. Each day the black and white in my life began to fade into vibrant color. Life was becoming saturated with happiness. Truth be told, I had a lot of paper to work through and needed a shredder to fit it all into one waste basket. As I worked through that, I began creating my own resources daily with the hope of helping more children than just the 30 to 100 students I got to teach every day. I wanted to touch *every* Maria in the world. I wanted my words and my resources to help her family build a better life for her. The *millionaire teacher mindset* really began as the *help a million Marias mindset*. First, I help all the Marias, and once I do that, I can begin helping all the teachers.

So that's what I did. I grabbed my old college laptop that seemed so "back to the future" that it barely turned on, and I started to create resources to sell online. In the first month I made $50, and I thought I had won the lucky teacher lottery.

"$50 dollars? This is basically enough money for Netflix and groceries."

That was the new internal dialogue I began having with myself as I pushed a little further each day. I found joy, passion, and purpose in selling my teaching resources, and it started a fire inside of me that engulfed my life like wildfire, and no amount of abundant ocean funk could put it out. Like most people with super exciting news to share, I shouted my newfound passion to all my teacher friends at school. But what I quickly encountered was a lot of negative Nancys and crabby Cindys. No one believed this was a real thing or even something that was obtainable. So I stopped sharing the good news gospel and began keeping my flaming happiness inside. Little did I know that each time I did that, I was building a hot inferno of happiness warriors that would carry this small-town southern girl into a blazing millionaire teacher.

That's the saucy and sexy secret to life, teachers. In this chapter I'm going to change your life but only if you believe I can. I will show you how to build a hot inferno of happiness warriors inside your mind that will carry you to the victory line to light your torch time and time again. It won't matter what the teacher next door says or even what those teachers on Instagram say because we—will—quiet—all—the—noise.

Those who conquer their millionaire teacher mindset conquer it all.

Let's start by fixing your limiting beliefs one step at a time.

Here's how limiting beliefs work. First, there's a random exciting thought that comes to your mind. "I think I can make a few extra dollars online." Next, there's a belief. "I'm probably too late to the game and the market is already completely saturated with thousands of teachers, so what's the use?"

Step 3 is the turning point of truth, and that's where I like to think of myself in a bright sparkling unicorn cape flying in to save the day. There are always tons of people doing other things before you, but there is only ONE version of you. No one can do it like you can do it. Truth be told, no one has seen YOU do it.

> There are always tons of people doing other things before you, but there is only ONE version of you. No one can do it like you can do it.

Think back to your favorite teacher of all time. Mine was Mr. David Van Wyk. He changed the game for me. My senior year of high school, I actually enjoyed English class, something that used to cause me anxiety. Walking into his classroom gave me hope again. He gave us time and space to write. He let my mind write things I had never known lived inside of me. He gave me courage to know that I could use my words on paper to do anything I wanted. He gave me the courage to know that I could write this book.

What if I had never had Van Wyk? *What if your students had never had you?*

Finally, there's the reality. If you can fix your mindset and conquer your limiting belief (step 2), then you can and you will earn a million dollars.

I'm living freakin' proof. Just saying.

Pause and Reflect

What is a limiting belief that is stopping you from pursuing your dreams?

So you're thinking great, I totally understand how limiting beliefs work now, but I really don't understand how to stop the noise inside my preprogrammed crabby head. The word millionaire isn't even in our language unless it's a total joke. Millionaires dress in tailored suits and spandex dresses. They wear leather loafers and five-inch pointed shoes. They wake up to hairstylist heroes and spray-tanned skin. They do not look like me, so what's the use?

The reason I know you're thinking those thoughts is that I am just like you. I've thought the same things about millionaires and lottery winners. I've watched the television shows where you get sucked in by people buying their dream home because they've finally struck it rich. I've drank too many glasses of wine with my husband and named the things we would purchase if we were to win that magical money number that we call a million dollars.

The steps I'm going to lay out for you in this chapter are worth more than money could ever buy. They are worth more than millions and more than billions. If you fix what's between your ears and behind your eyes, you will win.

The Millionaire Teacher Mindset

Step 1: Begin to Coach Yourself Using Your Own Internal Dialogue

It's easy to get caught up in what everyone else thinks. You will hear different voices and see different looks and stares. We are conditioned at a very early age to be apprehensive about the way we are perceived by others. I know for me, a small town southern girl from Georgia, this was one of the most difficult obstacles I had to get over, and that's why I put it first in the millionaire teacher mindset, because if we can get over the hurdle of "I hope everyone is okay with my decisions," we can tackle any and every challenge. This isn't a quick fix. You won't coach yourself overnight to think new thoughts. Just look at me, I am four years in the making teaching you this concept. It first started with pure determination to avoid negative banter every day.

As a classroom teacher, I began finishing my lesson plans and graded papers quickly, and instead of sitting in the lounge or in another classroom with my colleagues, I decided to take action. I began walking every day during my planning period and listened to podcasts that fueled my internal inferno. I began telling myself, "YES, I CAN," instead of "maybe I will." I didn't know for sure what the answer was yet, or what mountain I was going to climb to get to the highest peak in my lifetime, but I knew I was ready for the hike. Every day was a journey through a journey. My internal dialogue was fixed on fixing myself. It's funny how things change when you fix your mindset. I began fixing everything in my life. I started eating better and exercising more, and completely masked the old, dirty me.

Even if the chants I was saying in my head weren't my reality just yet, I knew they could happen. Each time I went into the teacher's bathroom, I would wash my hands and take a good, long, agonizing look at myself. And believe it or not, I'd say out loud: "Kayse, what do you want for your life? It's time to become the best version of yourself. You will change the lives of others. Do that."

You see what happened? I stopped relying on anyone else to change me and started relying on myself. I was my biggest supporter. I was my biggest cheerleader. I spoke kind words into my life each day, and they slowly began taking form in ways I never thought possible. Each goal then led to another bigger, more audacious goal. Each pep talk transformed into a self-made, soul-searching pep rally full of millions of raving fans and internal cheerleaders.

I stopped letting other people's negative vibrations affect me and started repelling each and every pulse that didn't feel like warm rays of sunshine beaming on my face. Let's say teachers were in a faculty meeting complaining about a new implementation we had to begin next week with reading-focused literacy goals. I'd smile, say "that sounds absolutely amazing," and walk back to my classroom unaffected by their negative banter. It began feeling so good that I started to make people uncomfortable. But remember, this isn't about them. This is about you. This is about your mindset. This is about your hopes and dreams of building a side hustle that surpasses your wildest imagination.

Step 2: Focus on Constant, Persistent Action Forward

Perhaps the most important part of the millionaire teacher mindset is the constant, persistent action forward. Our purpose can get diluted in our everyday routines and become muddy and difficult to find. We sometimes take giant steps forward only to get kicked giant leaps in the opposite direction. It's the promise of happiness that keeps us going during these undeniably difficult obstacles. It's like we are army crawling through the thick mud each day to chase this dream that seems light years ahead of us.

Just Keep Going.

Some days will be filled with rainbows and butterflies, while other days the rainbows are nowhere in sight and the torrential downpour of life is at our doorsteps.

Just Keep Going.

The only thing about this that's easy is knowing that it never is. Don't lose your focus. Don't forget that done is better than perfect and that constant, persistent action forward will get you to your dream of becoming a millionaire teacher.

You may dream of one day leaving the classroom forever or of becoming a rockstar teacher inside the classroom who never has to worry about money again. Either way, the dream is the same. Whatever your deepest desires are, never let them get too far from the forefront of your mind. When the cloud of doubt begins to creep in . . .

Just Keep Going.

Step 3: Surf on the Crest of the Wave

Throughout this entire book, you're learning strategies and tactics from the best teachers in the business. They've built empires on the side while still hustling inside the classroom. They've experienced the highest of highs and the lowest of lows. Living in the safe zone of life isn't in their wheelhouse. They've taken each wave of this trek and surfed on the crests as long as possible, but no wave ever stays at the crest forever. There will always be the trough of the wave.

The moment when things hit rock bottom. The moment when you ask yourself, "is this even worth it?"

That's normal. We all experience the trough of the waves, but it's our constant, persistent action forward that helps us surf on the crest for the longest possible time imaginable. Truth be told, in the beginning of this journey, each teacher may see more hang time at the bottom of the waves. It's what I like to call the hard work hustle—and, well, it's hard.

Some mornings you'll wake up at 4 AM to chase this dream, while other nights you'll stay up so late you'll see the dawn of morning coming through your windows.

All I can tell you is that it's worth it.

Keep surfing. Keep chasing that hang time. Each ride gets longer and better than the one before.

> Keep surfing. Keep chasing that hang time. Each ride gets longer and better than the one before.

Step 4: Prepare for the Trough of the Wave

Preparation is key for experiencing the trough of each wave. One of the key indicators of a successful teacherpreneur is the understanding that this is in fact a long game. None of the teachers in this book found quick success. It was a long way to get here.

Step 5: Work on Yourself Every Single Day

This step is the most important one in the entire millionaire teacher mindset process. It's one that takes the most work and most dedication of them all.

Sleep

It's seven to eight hours a day, teachers. That means if you want to wake up in the wee hours of the morning and conquer the day before your children wake up, you need to go to bed much earlier. Since math isn't my strongest trait, I'll let you guys figure out the equation for that.

Exercise

You can't be the best version of you without proper physical care. I used to think that going to the gym each day was the only way I could do proper exercise, but I was so wrong. I now exercise from the privacy of my own home through at-home workouts and am happier and stronger than ever.

Walking

Even though walking is a great form of exercise, I am categorizing it by itself in this list. I take an hour walk each day around lunch to clear my head. It helps me get an extra hour or so of quality work out of myself afterward. It's where I fuel my brain with podcasts and listen to countless audio books. I began my walking journey while I was still teaching. Each day during my planning period, I would escape briefly to get my walk in, and I began listening to podcasts that changed the trajectory of my life forever.

Reading

The very first personal development book I ever read was Stephen Covey's *The 7 Habits of Highly Effective People*. Life changing books inspire the mind and soul unlike anything I've ever tried to do for spiritual growth. They grab me and take me to a place where dreamers live. A place outside of my daily life where I can dream bigger dreams and chase higher highs. Some of my favorite books for building my mindset are:

> *Think and Grow Rich*
> *You Are a Badass at Making Money*
> *Dollars Flow to Me Easily*
> *Free to Focus*
> *Crushing It*
> *This Is Marketing*
> *High Performance Habits*
> *Shoe Dog*
> *Can't Hurt Me*

Pause and Reflect

How can you make time to sleep, exercise, and read more and improve your self-care?

Courses

It wasn't until I began spending thousands of dollars (yes, I mean thousands) on courses that I began seeing my true potential. There's something about the transformation inside of that expensive transaction that shifted my entire mindset. Those purchases were dollars invested in my brain and knowledge bank that will draw interest for a lifetime. Every course I have purchased has paid for itself 10-fold.

Do your research on courses to help build your business, and you will see your greatest potential unlocked. Work on yourself every single day and begin to form new habits that will release your inner millionaire teacher.

The best is yet to come.
I'll see you at the million.

8

Navigating Social Media for Your Side Hustle

Cynthia Frias

Did you know that one out of five teachers have taken a side hustle (*Education Week*, June 19, 2018)? As a solution to stagnant wages in their profession, educators are finding ways to supplement their income by using their expertise or interest. This chapter will provide you with helpful social media tips that you can use right away, whether you choose to stay within the educational world or enter another area.

My name is Cynthia, and I work with some of the biggest Instafamous educators. I help build their brand awareness, generate new leads, and gain new "real" followers. I will share straightforward and informative tips that you can start to implement immediately. I hope you find them useful.

With so much to learn and so little time, let's jump right into it.

Social Media: Where Do You Start?

Taking the first steps can be overwhelming. There are numerous platforms from which to choose. I recommend starting small and being selective. Pick one or two social media platforms. Master them first, then branch out.

Social Media Platforms Stats*

- *Facebook* is the biggest, with more than 2 billion users.
- *YouTube* users watch a billion hours of video every day.
- *Instagram* has 1 billion monthly active visitors.
- *Twitter* has 330 million users and is a source for things that are happening now.
- *LinkedIn* has 610 million users.
- *Pinterest* is the smallest, with 265 million users.

*Source: www.brandwatch.com/blog/amazing-social-media-statistics-and-facts/

How Often Should You Post?

While there is no magic formula, the general consensus seems to favor posting once a day. More importantly, be consistent and keep in mind that quality and knowing your audience is better than quantity. Here are some basic guidelines:

- *Instagram:* One to three times a day
- *Facebook:* At minimum, three times per week
- *Twitter:* Tweets have such a short span—minimum 10 times a day

Pro Tips:

- Make social media part of your daily routine. I personally post at the same time each day. Setting up an alarm on your phone can be extremely helpful.
- Create a calendar and include important dates such as social media holidays (i.e., #nationalreadingday).
- Use the same username across accounts if possible.
- Add social media follow buttons to your website.
- Study your analytics—see what post times work best.
- Review all your settings.
- Be human. Interact and respond to comments.

- Monitor everything, i.e., negative comments.
- Follow the 80/20 rule: 80% of our social media post should inform, educate, and entertain. Use the other 20% to promote your business.
- Don't engage with negative comments.
- Respond to all @mentions and comments.
- Learn your audience (age, female/male, where they live).

Pause and Reflect

How often do you currently post? How can you make it a part of your daily routine?

The Dos and Don'ts of Social Media for Teachers

It is normal for teachers to want to share inspiring events in their classrooms. But keep in mind a few things before doing so. Here are some tips:

- Know which students have opted out of image/video sharing. Protect their confidentiality.
- Be familiar with the district policy and share it with your students/parents.
- Consider having separate accounts, personal and professional ones. Different audience, different accounts.
- Don't share students' faces or names without parental consent.
- Blur faces and watch for reflections. There are several free apps you can use, or you can add an emoji over the face. Take inventory of anything in the classroom that may contain sensitive information. Looks for name tags or articles of clothing that may have a name on it.

◆ Ensure you review FERPA, the Family Educational Rights Privacy Act, and comply with the policy: https://www2.ed.gov/policy/gen/guid/fpco/ferpa/index.html.

◆ Don't post during school hours.

◆ Keep profiles clean.

◆ Do not geo-tag yourself with your school location.

◆ Pause before your post.

◆ Remember, screenshots can be taken easily, so think before your share.

◆ Know your privacy settings and become familiar with their limits.

Photography for Social Media

Visual content is key. As cliché as it sounds, a picture is worth a thousand words. It is essential to have clear, sharp images. There is a lot to learn in this area, but here are some of my favorite suggestions for making your social media pictures stand out.

◆ Know that with a smartphone you are basically set.

◆ Consider setting up a prop shelf for yourself.

◆ Go for natural lighting.

◆ Preferably take pictures right in front of a window for the diffused light effect.

◆ For backgrounds, solids work nicely and white matches everything. Try posterboards, bedding/fabric, wood tiles, and table tops.

Pro Tip:

Choose colors that match the branding of your website for fluid brand consistency.

Suggestions for Props:

+ Fairy lights or LED lights
+ Bubbles
+ Letterboards
+ Crayons/markers
+ Pens/pencils/rulers/scissors
+ Confetti (it is messy but awesome)
+ Buttons/ribbon/twine
+ Leaves/flowers/plants
+ Books/planners/magazines
+ Phones/phone cases/camera
+ Sunglasses/keys/purse
+ Sparklers (for selfies)
+ Holiday themes

Best Places to Find Inexpensive Props:

+ Candy stores
+ Dollar stores
+ Outdoors
+ Library books
+ Your desk
+ Craft/hardware stores
+ Garage/estate sales
+ Secondhand shops/flea markets
+ Family/friends

Tips for Setting Up the Flatlay:

+ Start with largest item as the base of your flatlay. Placement is trial and error.
+ Experiment with having items partially out of the frame.

- ◆ Create a nice mix of large and small.
- ◆ Work in diagonals. So if I put a color in the right corner, I will put another in the opposite lower corner.
- ◆ Organize and reorganize.
- ◆ Use sticky dots to keep items in place.
- ◆ Hover over the flatlay and get a good feel for the photo. Grab your camera/phone and check out how it looks inside the frame.
- ◆ Compositional tip: Use the S curve to place items, so if you are looking at all the items in the photo you could draw an S over them. Don't be afraid to just feature one item in the post. Portrait mode or highlight looks great. Take a square image and then take another to share to Stories.
- ◆ Focus on:
  - ◆ Brightness
  - ◆ Whiteness
  - ◆ Sharpness
  - ◆ Contrast
  - ◆ Saturation
  - ◆ Highlights
  - ◆ Shadow

This is your very own art. There is no wrong or right way. Be yourself and have fun. And remember that practice makes perfect. Invest some time in learning from free tutorials/resources available online.

Pause and Reflect

Which strategies resonated with you the most for improving your visual content?

The Best Time to Post on Social Media

Unfortunately, there are no perfect answers. However, there is enough data to share some suggestions.

- ◆ *Instagram*: Think off-work hours, such as weekends, lunch, and dinner. Avoid posting during working hours.
- ◆ *Facebook*: People tend to jump on when starting work, going online for the first time that day. Facebook sees an increase in clickthrough rates during lunch hours.
- ◆ *Twitter*: People use it regularly as a way to stay up-to-date with news, etc.
- ◆ *Pinterest*: Weekends tend to be the best time. Avoid posting when people are at work.

Head to your profile insight and look around. Become familiar with the information provided and adjust as needed.

Understanding the Algorithms

The algorithm plays a huge role in social media success. It is the way the platforms sort posts based on their relevance to users. It is definitely worth staying informed of the latest updates and changes. Take time to search for new articles or view the latest video to stay current on the algorithm world. Facebook CEO Mark Zuckerberg has described an algorithm approach that prioritizes "meaningful social interaction," which includes liking pics, commenting, replying to comments, and sharing. It is crucial to focus on engagement. Think of it like a holiday party. Welcome and encourage engagement. Create content that sparks a conversation. Ask a question, ask followers to tag a friend in a post or to double tap if they like the post, etc. Number one tip: You need to engage with other people. This is what the algorithm wants to see. It may be exhausting, but it is worth the energy.

The Ultimate List of What to Post on Social Media

Coming up with daily post ideas can be exhausting. The number one tip I can give is to write captions that engage. And remember that the first line is what people see first before clicking, so make it stand out. Here are some ideas:

- Flatlay images
- Quotes/tips/fun fact graphics
- Giveaways
- Behind the scenes (your desk)
- Throwbacks/flashbacks/vintage posts
- Weekly roundups
- Sneak peeks
- Selfies
- Thank-you graphics
- Customer reviews
- Highlights from your city
- National social media holiday posts
- Lifestyle content such as your classroom
- Reposts of someone else's content (Always give photo credit. Simply tagging someone in the photo is not enough.)
- Carousels/slides for showcasing collections
- Collaborations with influencers in your niche (Start with lower-count influencers at first.)
- Takeovers
- Live videos
- Customer photos (They build credibility, but always ask for permission first and give proper photo credit. Be inventive. Remind your followers how they can be featured by tagging your brand.)
- VIDEO IS HUGE. Don't forget Boomerangs.
- Picture collages

Creating Catchy Captions

Coming up with content can be challenging. Here are some suggestions:

- Asking questions
- Sharing fun facts
- Writing one-word captions
- Sharing something personal
- Using emojis
- Posting song lyrics
- Asking followers to tag a friend
- Asking followers to double tap if they agree
- Posting quotes or something humorous (Visuals are worth a thousand words.)
- Sharing your knowledge/expertise with a helpful tip
- Reposting—sharing someone else's content (Always give proper credit and when in doubt, ask.)
- Sharing a #tbt (#ThrowbackThursday)
- Thanking your followers and/or asking them to share your brand
- Creating a short video or Boomerang (There has been an explosion of it in recent years, and it will definitely attract your audience. "I see video as a megatrend," said Facebook CEO Mark Zuckerberg in February 2017.)
- Posting something seasonal or a national holiday graphic
- Showing off positive customer feedback

Pro Tip:

Use third-party apps such as IG LineBreak to create clean line breaks in your captions.

The Importance of Hashtags

Including hashtags (#) in your post helps categorize content for your audience. More importantly, it allows you to reach a larger audience. Otherwise, you are just sharing to your current followers. And of course, the more hashtags you use, the bigger the audience. However, it is crucial that you mix them up to avoid looking spammy. Looking spammy will decrease your reach. There are free apps that can help you find the best hashtags for your niche, such as Tag Blender. A time-saving tip is to create multiple groups of hashtags in your notes. Copy and paste, but make sure you are not using the same ones repeatedly.

Hashtag Tips:

- ◆ Keep them relevant.
- ◆ Incorporate hashtags into your caption.
- ◆ If you have a brand #, encourage others to use it.
- ◆ Study hashtags used by like-minded businesses.
- ◆ Use specific hashtags.
- ◆ Add hashtags to your bio.
- ◆ Use low-density hashtags to increase visibility (find small to medium ones in your niche, allowing you to stay on an explorer's page longer).
- ◆ Sweet spot for hashtags: 5,000 to 500,000 posts.
- ◆ Avoid spammy hashtags like #followme.
- ◆ Use free third-party apps like Instagram Generator to find new hashtags for your niche.
- ◆ How many do you use?
  - ◆ *Twitter*: One hashtag.
  - ◆ *Instagram*: Up to 30.
  - ◆ *Facebook*: With the ever-changing algorithm, it is hard to say, but studies show that hashtagged Facebook

posts do worse than untagged ones. If you choose to add one or two, make sure it is relevant to the post. Avoid #likeforlike #followme tags.

◆ *YouTube*: Add hashtags in the titles and description to improve search.
◆ *Pinterest*: The only place to use/click on a hashtag is in the description.

Making the Most of Your Bio

Your bio must explain your business and what it offers.

◆ *Instagram*: You have 30 characters for your tagline, 150 for your description, and one clickable. Use the name field to share your top targeted words. Words included here are searchable. Capitalize the name section on your bio to optimize search results. Add any special skills, such as #readingspecialist. Adding #'s or @ in the bio makes it clickable on some platforms.
◆ *Facebook*: Make sure you fill out the "About" section completely and add a story that explains how your business ticks.
◆ *Twitter*: Bios allow a maximum of 160 characters. Use them cleverly.

Pro Tip:

What is a call to action? That is a phrase you will hear often. It is a way to entice your audience to take action. Use any and all buttons that allow for this. Optimize your picture/cover photos. Make sure your profile image is high resolution. Consider using your face.

Creating a Beautiful Feed

One sure way to convert your visitors into followers is to have a cohesive and beautiful feed. Since it is the first thing visitors will see, take time to plan. Select a color, theme, and style. Ask yourself: Do I prefer pastels, bright colors, or darker colors, or am I a minimalist? Chose the same filter and stick with it. The main rule is to stay consistent. There are many third-party apps that can help you with this. You might want to try creating an Instagram grid layout. Try a checkerboard grid, which consists of two themes—for example, a picture then a quote. Columns are created by posting a solid graphic for every third picture. A rainbow feed requires you to group like colors. Research this topic to find tutorials.

If you have a post that is not doing great on Instagram, or a particular photo that is not keeping things clean looking and professional, you can hide it instead of deleting it. You do that by using the archive/unarchive feature on Instagram. You can always bring it back if need be.

Pro Tip:

Think about color psychology when selecting a color theme. Blue is one of the most-used colors. Have you noticed how Facebook, PayPal, Capital One, and Twitter use blue? It is definitely worth the time to read up on this subject.

Wrapping Things Up

Hopefully this chapter has shed light on the basics of starting out with social media. While I realize side hustle marketing may not be high on the priority list, I do hope these tips and information will allow you to get the most out of social media with the limited time you have after work and home life.

Remember, social media is here to stay. It is free and accessible to most everyone. Maximize its use and work on building relationships. I like to think of social media in terms of collaboration over competition. You will be pleasantly surprised to find out how much like-minded businesses are willing to do for you. With that said, it's important to reciprocate if asked. There is no denying that it will be a lot of trial and error. But then look at it as a mistake, take it as an opportunity to grow, and learn from it. Don't overwhelm yourself—start slowly. You will notice over time how much easier it gets. However, be aware that social media changes often, so stay informed.

> I like to think of social media in terms of collaboration over competition. You will be pleasantly surprised to find out how much like-minded businesses are willing to do for you.

Let's Recap

Remember to narrow down your audience. Ask yourself, who is my customer? Choose one or two platforms to begin. Start small and be selective. Set up a goal/strategy and stick to it. Set up your calendar and establish set times to post. Quality is always more important than quantity. Perfect your images. Believe me, your followers will appreciate the work. Use tools/apps and especially analytics. Learn the demographic and see what posts are really working for you. Show that you are human and care by responding promptly. Use their first name in the caption if available. Be aware of trends. Don't be afraid to boost a post.

> Quality is always more important than quantity. Perfect your images. Believe me, your followers will appreciate the work.

Final Tips:

- ◆ Error messages: Many of us run to Twitter if Instagram is down. But you can also trust apps like Downdetector to tell you whether there are any current issues.
- ◆ Take time to learn all the available features on the different platforms. For example, Instagram Stories is a feature that allows users to share photos and videos that disappear after 24 hours.
- ◆ Use all available features such as geolocation for a greater reach.
- ◆ Search the top hashtag in your niche. Engage with those posts, leaving comments. However, skip the simple "Love" comment and be authentic.
- ◆ Research the right tools/apps to elevate your social media game.
- ◆ Keep an eye on the competition and learn from them. They give great inspiration and are probably doing the same things.
- ◆ Use the shopping features available on the different platforms.
- ◆ Be aware of phrases/images that may offend.
- ◆ If approached by big brands to be a "social media influencer" for their product or services, make sure to consider whether the endorsement aligns with your educational philosophy and niche. You don't want to end up in an unfollow zone.

9

Switching Lenses

Eric Crouch

"Eric, if you want to sit with the adults, you have to earn your place at the table."
—Uncle Johnny

Sitting at the table with the adults as an equal was a defining moment for me. No longer was I nephew or grandson; I was Eric. As the night carried on, I eventually found myself at the center of the conversation around my photography business. My seat at the table was sealed, but with that new position, I felt the need to have success stories to share. Regretfully, I was clueless about how to make the business happen.

For me photography is a creative outlet, a passion. I wanted to share my art, and I was shocked that people wanted to pay me for it. I grew up thinking that I wasn't artistic because I was told art was only drawing, painting, singing, or playing an instrument, not photography. I was a natural with the camera. So what happened? How did I become a teacher with a side hustle?

What wasn't revealed in the Thanksgiving dinner conversation was that our photography business was getting underway at the same time that college was wasting a ton of my time. There was really nothing else I needed to learn in school to be successful. Experience is the school we need, and the learning comes in the form of mistakes that teach us to do better. I was not going to experience any of this sitting in class, so I withdrew from all my first semester classes my junior year, but I kept the student loan money and used it to buy some new gear. Clearly that was a poor choice, but not as poor as repeating it all over again and dropping my GPA to a 1.7 by the beginning of what should have been my senior year. I was so concerned about proving to everyone else that I could be successful that I only fooled myself. Well, and my parents, who had no idea I had eight WFs (Withdraw Fails) and had pocketed all of the student loan money that year.

A few months later, I told my fiancée what I had done. She was less than thrilled and insisted that I either go back to school and get a degree or find a new fiancée. I decided that she was more important than my business, and if it made her feel uncomfortable, I would not drop out. A few weeks later, my grandfather passed away, and I knew I wasn't going back to school for business. The time had come to find something that was worth having and worth selling. I began to think about the injustices I could try and work towards improving, and I kept coming back to the same topic—teaching. I thought about my younger brother who hated school and spent many hours after school getting help. I knew my brother was brilliant because he grew up next to me. He was very bright but, for whatever reason, he struggled in school. His teachers weren't giving him what he needed. That, along with my own personal experience of not being guided or shown opportunities, led me to become a teacher. I knew that I never saw myself as creative in school because I couldn't dance, sing, draw, or play an instrument. I knew that if education were done properly, it was worth having. I decided I would re-enroll that upcoming fall and become a teacher.

Upon arriving at the registrar's office, I was notified that I was on academic probation. It turns out that when a student withdraws from two semesters, the school frowns upon it. My GPA was an impressive 1.7, so I scheduled an appointment with the dean of education to inform him that I was going to be a teacher and that I wanted to know what I needed to do to make it happen. For whatever reason, I was granted this meeting. He informed me that my WFs were going to cost me an additional year, that I would need to raise my GPA to the minimum 2.75, and that it would take at least four more years before I graduated. I retook those awful classes and graduated four years later at the top of my class. I have since been recognized nationally and internationally for my work in the classroom. Grades were just a number, and my story proves that.

Now, about the side hustle. I love photography in a different way than I love teaching. For me, pursuing two passions is important. I love teaching because of what I can do for others that no one did for me, but photography is something I do for myself.

Being True to You

To be clear, photography is a way for me to bring things to my classroom. It is not my way out of the classroom. I love being in the classroom, and photography gives me some choices that teaching alone cannot provide. Although photography is a more personal and creative passion for me, it also opens doors financially. I can do things inside and outside of my classroom that are only possible with a secondary income. Side hustles give you options, and there is nothing wrong with having options.

When I was in elementary school, it was clear that I did not fit in as a creative or as a creator. In our traditional public school system, students were limited to a handful of art or music courses. Other creative expressions or explorations were not valued, taught, or explored. Looking back, it's clear how much of a tragedy this is because if I had the chance to pick up a camera in school, life would have made more sense and maybe, just maybe, I would have felt valued for the way I think and create. I am a divergent thinker with learning and attention issues, which often do not align with traditional classroom work. Yes, my worksheet attention span is about 10 seconds on a good day.

Like so many other diverse learners, I was put on ADHD medicine at a young age, and my dosages increased as school became more difficult. I was forced to take more medicine so I could "pay attention" and fit into a world that didn't fit me. Part of my drive to make the classroom a place for my learners, and not a place where I teach, comes from the awful feeling I experienced from being marginalized as a learner. No one reached out and tried to make things work for me. School and society norms declared that it was my fault that I wasn't learning. And if I wasn't paying attention or learning, more medicine needed to be prescribed. My parents and my teachers were navigating uncharted waters, and the medicine seemingly made me more compliant and seemed to be the easiest solution available.

When I put in the extra year of retaking those business classes, I was highly motivated because I was passionate about helping students. I knew I could be a resource to those students sitting in classrooms who aren't seen as valuable or talented because their teachers lack understanding of how they learn. I learned how to cope with my learning and attention issues, and I knew I could share those revelations with my students. More importantly, I understood that finding a passion intrinsically motivated me to learn and gave me the motivation to pay attention and focus on things I did not care about (business school), so that I could get closer to my passion of helping students.

Life is short, and every person deserves the chance to explore more than one passion. You deserve to find your purpose inside and outside of the classroom. Photography gives me a creative joy that then adds to my teaching and helps me grow as a person. I just happen to make money and have options because of it. I don't do it because I can make money; I do it because I can make a better me. I learn more about myself and my abilities when I push myself and tackle challenges that are beyond the challenges of yesterday. This training, if you will, has prepared me for the classroom where every day is different. We get one chance to make a difference, and our students get one chance in our class. We have to be prepared to give them the learning opportunities that will help them grow and become better versions of themselves.

Needs Assessment

I remember laying in the field for seven hours waiting for a sniper to take a shot. I couldn't move or make a noise. He was trained for his role, but I certainly wasn't trained for this. We were on Ft. Benning, doing a simulated combat mission photoshoot, and my objective was to capture the essence of the training. I wasn't there to take a staged photo; I was there to create a feeling through capturing a photo that represented and embodied what it means to be a sniper. I waited and waited, ready to capture gun fire at any second. Seven hours passed and he never fired his weapon. I got great shots in the process, and I was able to sell those photos as a civil service contractor for the U.S. military, but what I didn't realize was that I could go seven hours without going to the bathroom. I was training to be a teacher when teaching wasn't even on my horizon. Sometimes the thing you wait all day, all week, or all month for is not the actual thing you need. What you really needed was right in front of you.

As a business owner, it's easy to project these needs and convince yourself of some. And many of those needs come at a cost. It is critical that you learn to negotiate with yourself. Just because you have an idea doesn't always mean you need to act on it. There may be a less attractive but more practical solution staring you in the face. When I was dreaming about capturing the essence of a sniper, I thought it meant I needed to get this beautiful moment where the trigger is pulled and the bullet could be seen leaving the barrel. Instead, the true essence of a sniper is not to shoot but to scout, be patient and if, necessary, engage. The simple, less attractive things are usually more practical and more attainable but do not draw us in like the "needs" we convince ourselves of. Learn to negotiate with yourself and make sure you explore options that don't involve taking on debt first.

Pause and Reflect

What are the "needs" you have convinced yourself of?
What is the one piece of equipment that would be a game changer if you had it?
What are you willing to give up to get that piece of equipment?
Are you sure you want to sacrifice savings or money meant for your family?

Remember, learning to negotiate with yourself means that you must be willing to give something to get something. Make a plan and stick with it. Make sure you bounce ideas off loved ones who could be impacted, and make sure that they are on board.

The Rubber Ball

Imagine life as a game in which you are juggling five balls in the air. You name them—work, family, health, friends and spirit—and you're keeping all of these in the air. You will soon understand that work is a rubber ball. If you drop it, it will bounce back. But the other four balls—family, health, friends and spirit—are made of glass. If you drop one of these, they will be irrevocably scuffed, marked, nicked, damaged or even shattered. They will never be the same. You must understand that and strive for balance in your life.

—Bryon Dyson

Life is a juggling act. Sometimes you find yourself juggling different things—some things you signed up for and some things you didn't. That doesn't change the fact that you feel like you need to keep all of those things in the air.

Treat Your Business Like a Cousin, Not a Baby

One of the first things I was told by our accountant was to treat a business like it is your baby. At the time my business partner and I were not sure what to think about that, so we just split everything in thirds. I got a third, he got a third, and the business got a third. I am pretty sure it was the worst advice we ever received. It shifted our mindset from doing the work we love, to working solely to cover bottom line. Originally, we did not have a studio or a place to rent. We met folks locally to save costs, and we used the business third to pay our taxes and the cost of materials. Everything came back to numbers, and those numbers influenced our decisions.

This was unhealthy, and my hope is that you will think of your opportunity as more of a cousin than a baby. A cousin is someone who can be close and far away at the same time. A baby needs constant attention, and for two business partners with young families, we didn't have time to be raising a side baby. I wish we had never listened to that man; I wish we had simply split everything 50/50 and stayed the course doing work that mattered to us. Eventually, we rented a space that ate away more of our profits. We took on additional work that was not aligned with our vision because we needed to cover costs. We put the baby first and did what we had to do to make sure it was healthy at all times, even if it meant it was unhealthy for us and our families. Luckily, my partner and I married spouses who are better than we deserve. They allowed us to try, and they still supported us when it was tough. Life is going to feel complicated regardless, but when you add a business, it is a rubber ball that will bounce back. Your family and health are fragile. So if you are going to drop one, make sure you drop the one that will bounce back.

Pause and Reflect

What are the major moving parts in your life?
What are the things you can allow to hit the floor that
may come back later?

Enough With Faking It Until You Make It

I think my business partner and I would do a lot differently if we could do it all over again. One thing would be to cut out more of "the perception is reality" or "fake it 'til you make it" mindset. Stop with the fake it 'til you make it. You are not going to fool your bank account, and you aren't going to fool your family or the ones you love. Running a business and working for yourself isn't about trying to create a mirage of success to push on other people. It's about setting and reaching goals and pursuing a purpose. As I tell my students, once all the fluff settles, there is nothing left but work, and the only thing keeping you from getting to where you are to where you want to be is you.

> If you must compare, compare your effort to your success. Do not compare your success or lack of success to someone else's effort.

If you must compare, compare your effort to your success. Do not compare your success or lack of success to someone else's effort.

Learn to Say NO!

I like to wake up early and get my work done first thing or finish work after everyone goes to sleep. That seems obvious, but then those phone calls and emails sneak up on you, and that is what really makes this tough. It's easy to get sucked into your phone, and it's even easier if you are working on something business-related because you will try and justify it. I remember thinking that if I didn't reply quickly, I was going to lose money. And if I lost money, that could mean lost future opportunities, which my family wouldn't want. I remember telling my wife that I had to always be available. This couldn't be further from the truth. In fact, the opposite is true. The more available I am, the more people will take advantage of that, and you will end up creating a world of work.

I remember being without cell phone service one afternoon and how nervous I was that I might miss a new opportunity. My daughter came over and asked, "Daddy, when you're done, will you come play with me?" That was the moment I realized I was missing out on my life as dad. I had blurred the home and work boundaries so much that work was eating my every moment.

When you have a side hustle, it's easy to lose sight of the boundary between home and work. Many times you are working at home, which can create a lot of issues. When I was photo editing at home, my family was under the impression that I was freely available and should be spending time with them. I wish someone would have warned me ahead of time how important these boundaries are and that being open about them is essential to keeping everyone on the same page.

Saying no is probably the best thing you can do to create some boundaries.

Everyone is not your customer.

♦ If your customer cannot wait for you to eat dinner with your family, they aren't your customer.
♦ If your customer cannot wait until after your child's baseball game, they aren't for you.

I think you get where this is going. Work for your goals, not for the dollar. It's okay to say no, and it may be the hardest thing to say. But saying no is important because not everyone is a good fit for you or your

> Saying no is important because not everyone is a good fit for you or your business. Nothing is worth the price of your family or your own mental health.

business. Nothing is worth the price of your family or your own mental health. Find customers who have the same values as you do and who aren't going to cross those boundaries.

Pause and Reflect

Have you ever crossed the boundary between work and home?
Are you willing to turn off your phone when you get home?
Are you willing to let that customer wait until Monday?

River People and Pie People

Success can often reveal things about the people who are around you. So what is a river person and what is a pie person?

A river person is someone who sees success as a flowing river. Anyone can go and take from the river, and there is plenty for everyone.

A pie person is someone who sees success as a pie. The piece that you take is no longer available for them.

Both types of people are in our buildings, and that probably has less to do with you than with them. But it can be challenging to navigate nonetheless. Not everyone will be cheering for your success and nor will everyone see the value in what you do. Here is the good news: That's okay. Just like everyone is not going to be the right customer, not everyone is going to like your Facebook page and share all of your posts. Those people are not your people anyways, and you might realize it's time to part ways. Don't give a lot of time and energy to those folks, but rather consider finding the people who are on your side and who do want to work with you. The internet has made the world much smaller. Whether you are a photographer, a baker, or a Teachers Pay Teachers seller, you can connect to people who are beyond your neighborhood and talk shop with people who aren't threatened by you or your business.

Finding your people makes what you do even more enjoyable. It's easy to get caught up in the day-to-day running of a business, which can cause you to forget that you do need some time for yourself. Chances are that your family may not be too interested in talking shop. Your family wants you to be you. An Instagram friend, on the other hand, can become a great supporter and encourager while helping you problem solve and navigate something they may have previously experienced. If you don't have someone you can grab a cup of coffee with in your immediate circles, don't be afraid to search and explore others on Instagram, Twitter, or Facebook.

Your people are out there. Finding a friend who mentors you is a breath of fresh air. And do not forget that there may be an opportunity for you to help someone navigate challenges that you figured out. It's hard to expect to find help and answers to things, if you aren't willing to be that person for someone else. Could they take that information and use it? Sure, but aren't you wanting the same thing for that same purpose? Don't hate on pie people and then become one. There is plenty of work for all of us. Be a great sharer, and it will pay you back in ways you can never imagine.

> There is plenty of work for all of us. Be a great sharer, and it will pay you back in ways you can never imagine.

Pause and Reflect

Who are the pie and river people in your life?
Which one would others classify you as?
Are you intentionally networking and making connections in your space?
What will you do tomorrow to invest in someone else the way you want someone to invest in you?

Life is more complicated with a side hustle, but also more interesting. I hope you will consider some of the things you read in this chapter and the incredible tips throughout this handbook as you navigate your business. I hope you will set some boundaries upfront, make something worth having, and remember that it is okay to have more than one passion. And it's also okay to make money doing it. Life is a lot like a camera. You are constantly switching lenses and changing settings, trying to capture each moment with the right settings and lens. Sometimes you miss the shot, and sometimes you nail it! Just don't give up. Keep going and remember that the only thing keeping you from what you want is you.

Continue the Conversation

We hope the stories and advice in this book have inspired you to go out and start a side hustle or tweak one that you already have in the works. Good luck on your journey, and don't forget to stay connected with us on Instagram @sidehustlehandbook. Thank you for all you do to make a difference in education!